D1094972

PEOPLES ON THE MOVE

The Overseas Chinese

Hugh Baker

B.T. Batsford Ltd, London

Contents

Typeset by Tek-Art Ltd, Kent
and printed in Great Britain by
R J Acford Ltd,
Chichester, Sussex
for the publishers
B.T. Batsford Ltd
4 Fitzhardinge Street
London W1H 0AH

ISBN 0 7134 5426 1

Frontispiece
Young coolies in the late nineteenth century.

Acknowledgments

I would like to thank my colleagues at the School
of Oriental and African Studies for their help: Paul
Fox for preparing the illustrations; Sue Harrop for
her skill in drawing the maps; Rosemary Seton for
locating archive material; and particularly Carol
Maynard for her patience in typing the
manuscript.

Foreword

Throughout history people have been on the move from one place to another. In this way a large part of the world has become inhabited. For most of human history people moved in small groups, searching for new lands where they could live free from enemies and hunger.

The greatest migration, or movement, of people occurred between 1820 and 1930 and was made possible by the development of the railway and the steam ship. During that period millions of people made the long journey from Europe to America, but also to Australia and New Zealand, and from European Russia eastwards into Siberia. Smaller movements of people also took place in Asia, with Chinese moving into the lands and islands of Southeast Asia and Japanese out into the Pacific and to America.

Most people moved as a result of what can crudely be described as a mixture of "push" and "pull" factors. They were "pushed" out of their homes by poor living conditions, shortage of land, or lack of religious and political freedoms, and "pulled" or attracted to new lands and countries by the hope of a better way of life and new opportunities. For some people migration was largely involuntary: either they did not want to move or they had very little choice. Between 1520 and 1870 millions of Africans were forcibly taken across the Atlantic to America as slaves, and today there are millions of refugees in the world who have been compelled to leave their homes because of war, famine and disease.

Migration mixes people together, not only people from different parts of the same country but also peoples of different languages and cultures. Countries such as the United States and Brazil have been created by people from vastly different backgrounds. And if we look closely at the history of Britain we will see that our language and culture have been shaped by migrants coming to these islands during the last thousand years or more. Migration from Europe to the new lands after 1700 led to the spread of languages (English and Spanish to the Americas, for example), the development of new accents and new cultures, or ways of life.

The aim of this series of books is to look at different examples of "peoples on the move" – why did they leave their original homes? How did they travel? What did they take with them? What did they find in the new lands? How did they settle down? What were relations like between "natives" and newcomers? And what was the impact of new economic systems on the land?

If you have had the experience of moving home, perhaps from one country to another, or even from one place to another *within* a country, then you may be able to share the feelings of people who migrated in the past. If you have never moved home then perhaps these books will help you to understand the reasons why people move, and why in the world today there are, for example, people of European origin living in America and South Africa, and people of African and Asian origin living also in America and in Britain.

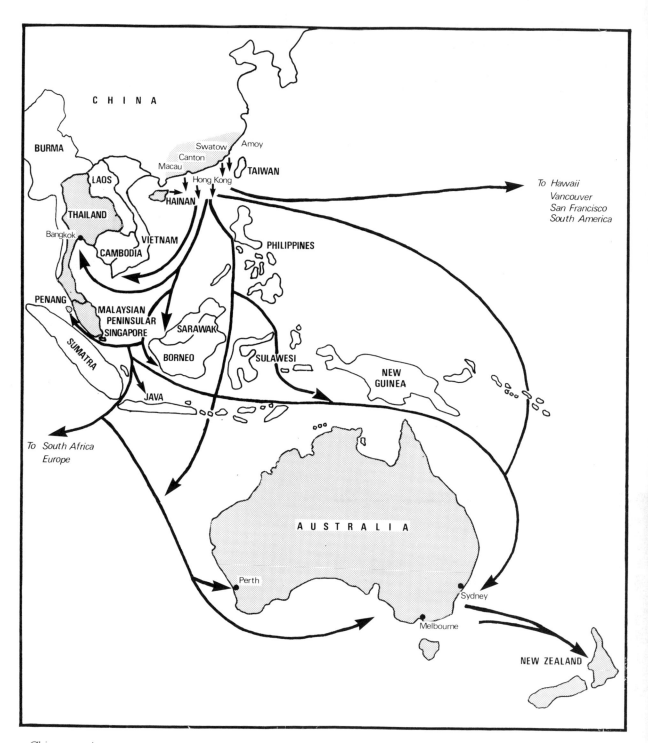

Chinese emigrant routes.

1 Quong Tart: a Chinese Success Story

In 1859 a nine-year-old Chinese boy made the long sea voyage from his home in South China to Sydney in Australia. He travelled with an uncle who was going to seek his fortune on the newly discovered gold-fields. Together they trekked inland to the mining town of Braidwood, and there young Quong Tart was set to work in Thomas Forsyth's store.

He quickly learned to speak the same kind of English as Forsyth, who was a Scotsman, and for the rest of his life Quong Tart had a Scottish accent. While serving in the store he became friendly with an Australian couple called Pierce and Alice Simpson, and they took him to live with them. When he was 14 they gave him a gold claim, and he was lucky enough to strike gold on it.

By the time he was 21 Quong Tart was already quite rich. He dressed in smart Western clothes, played cricket, went horse-racing, dined on

Quong Tart in 1887. With him are two Chinese officials in full robes. They had been sent to Australia by the Chinese Emperor to find out what living conditions were like for their countrymen there.

haggis, and acted as interpreter for the other Chinese miners. His own level of education was high and he helped to build a school for the children of miners. In 1871 he became a British citizen. When he went back to visit his home town in China ten years later he went as a very successful landowner, businessman and public figure:

He visited his mother in China (causing much amazement there by his insistence on wearing European clothes and rejecting any Chinese girl for wife), returned to Sydney, eventually (in 1886) to marry a Liverpool girl called Margaret Scarlett, and remained a leader of the Chinese merchant class in Sydney and a prominent figure in charitable affairs, both Chinese and Australian.
(C.A. Price, *The Great White Walls are Built*, Canberra, 1974, p. 221)

Quong Tart was strongly opposed to opium-smoking. In 1883 he organized a petition of 4000 signatures to try to stop the import of opium into Australia. The petition was not blocked by the Chinese, but by the Premier of New South Wales, who was worried that the colony would lose tax income if the opium trade was stopped.

Until his death in 1903 Quong Tart was tireless in his efforts to promote understanding between the Australians and the Chinese. He organized public lectures, helped to settle disputes, and talked constantly with leaders of both communities. His personal charm, intelligence and fluent command of both Chinese and English made him ideal for this role. As we shall see in a later chapter, it was not an easy task he had set himself.

Quong Tart was just one among many millions of Chinese who went abroad to make a living. He was very successful indeed, but most of his countrymen had a much harder time. Before we look at what their life overseas was like, we will try to understand the life in China which they had left.

2 China Fills up

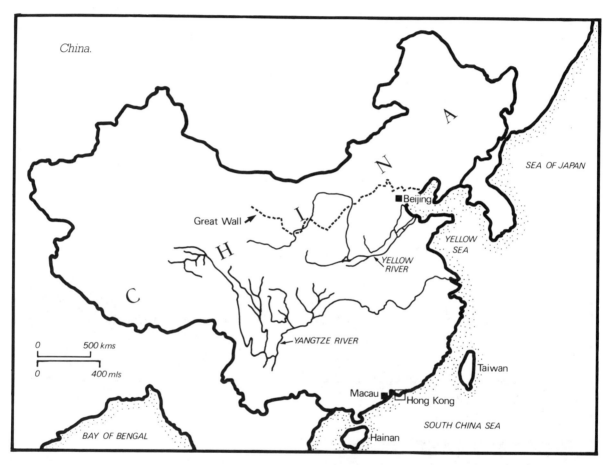

China.

Great Wall

YELLOW RIVER

YELLOW SEA

SEA OF JAPAN

Beijing

YANGTZE RIVER

Taiwan

Macau
Hong Kong

SOUTH CHINA SEA

Hainan

BAY OF BENGAL

0   500 kms

0   400 mls

The Chinese people have not always lived all over China as they do now. Four thousand years ago they were to be found only in a small area in the north of the country. Here they farmed the yellow powdery soil known as *loess*, the same soil which washes down the streams and gives its colour to the great Huang He, the Yellow River.

The rest of China was the home of many other peoples, who spoke different languages and had quite different customs and dress from the Han Chinese.

The peoples who lived to the north of China were fierce and unfriendly. So hostile were they that eventually, from about 300 B.C. onwards, the

Chinese built walls to keep them from invading. In less than a hundred years a great wall was built right across China's northern border, and when it was finished it stretched 1400 miles from east to

Yellow was important for the Chinese because it is the colour of earth. Earth is vital to the farmer, and the Chinese are, above all, farmers. So yellow was the colour of importance. It was the colour of the Emperor's clothes and of the roofs of his palace in Beijing, the huge Forbidden City, which has yellow roofs to this day.

west. Not only did it keep attackers out, it also kept the Chinese in. It reminded them that it was pointless to go further north, where the soil was not good for farming and the climate was severe.

As the Chinese increased in power and numbers they added to the land under their control, but it was always southwards that they spread. When they moved into a new area they conquered or drove away the other peoples who were living there. By 2000 years ago the population was about 60 million and there were already some Chinese settlements on the southernmost coast of China. More or less all of what is called "China proper" was occupied by Chinese people in the next thousand years, and the population rose to over 100 million.

It was not only the rise in the number of people which made the Chinese move. Drought and

Han Chinese

Sometimes the Chinese call themselves "Men of Han" or "The Han". For 400 years, until A.D. 200, the Han dynasty ruled China. It was a time of great glory and progress, and people are proud to use the name still.

Non-Han peoples

There are still 54 different "minority peoples" living in China today. The Mongolians and Tibetans are two of the better-known but others have names like Miao, Yi, Uygur, Yao, Hani, Lahu, Bai and Zhuang. Some of these groups are very large – there are over 12 million Zhuang, for instance – and some number only a few thousand. Altogether, they amount to over 50 million out of a total population of 1100 million.

Walls

The earliest walls were made to keep different groups of unfriendly Chinese apart, but in the end it was more important to try to keep out the wild tribes and so the Great Wall was built. It varied in height from place to place and was made of different materials, some parts being of stone, others of brick, and much of it of pounded earth. Hundreds of thousands of soldiers and prisoners were used to build it. They were cruelly treated and those who died were buried under the wall. Many people used to believe that the dead bodies helped to make the wall strong.

The Great Wall of China north of Beijing. Some parts have been recently restored, others are tumble-down.

A farmer ploughs with the help of his water buffalo – a scene unchanged for centuries. Most farmers will not eat water buffalo meat or beef because they say it comes from the animals which are their farming friends.

famine were all too common in the north, and from time to time they were so bad that people left their homes to look for better lives in the south, where the climate was kinder and rainfall more reliable.

Worse than the weather were the savage roving tribesmen who lived north of the Great Wall. All through China's history these peoples looked greedily at the wealth and comfortable settled life of the Chinese. Whenever they were strong enough they would break through the Great Wall and attack China. Sometimes they were able to conquer large parts of the country, and then the Chinese people would flee from them. And, of course, it was always necessary to go south because the attackers came from the north.

The greatest moves south came in the fourth and twelfth centuries. In A.D. 317 Tartar tribes invaded, and about two thirds of the Han population fled to the south across the Yangzi River. In A.D. 1126 the Mongols under Genghis Khan came sweeping down through the country, and hordes of Chinese refugees again went southward.

Even in the twentieth century the same kind of movements have taken place. Refugees have fled from civil war, from Japanese invasion and from famine, and many of them have gone south. Here is part of a Chinese story written in 1932:

There were more than fifty of them striding along the narrow mud track. It was a grey morning, a north wind had sprung up during the night, and some said it was going to snow. But they couldn't stay any longer in that village. . . .

Their journey hadn't just begun a few days before – it was six months ago that their lands had been flooded and their entire year's harvest washed away. Then an army had passed through their village and stolen whatever else they had and set fire to their houses. All anyone had left were a few clothes, his empty hands and his life. Hunger and cold drove them like whips on their backs. And so, weeping, they left their village.
(Ba Jin, *Wu-shi-duo-ge*, Beijing, 1932)

In the civil war in China which raged from 1946 to 1949 the Communist armies had their base area in the north. As they gained the upper hand they pushed the retreating Nationalist forces under Chiang Kai Shek further and further south. Eventually the Nationalists crossed the water to the island of Taiwan. At the same time, floods of refugees also went south and found shelter in the British colony of Hong Kong and the Portuguese territory of Macau. The movement of the Chinese people was following its traditional direction.

3 Life in China

The life of the Chinese people was often hard, but the country as a whole was prosperous and civilized. Most people were farmers – even today four out of every five people in China work on the land.

To own and farm his own land was the dream of almost every man in China, and when he died his son would take over to carry on the work. The family became tied to the land which fed it, and a strong sense of pride in the land and of family pride developed.

In the family the men were treated as more important than the women. The father was the head of the family and his wife and his children and grandchildren were all expected to obey him. The father hoped that when his sons got married they would not leave to start a new home – instead, their wives would come to live with them in their father's house – but when daughters got married they would leave home to join their husbands. A man could have more than one wife, but a woman could only have one husband. Men could divorce their wives, but a wife could not divorce her husband.

Usually it was the men who worked in the fields and the women who did the housework. It was thought to be a waste of time and money to educate women who were just going to spend their lives in the house. Before the twentieth century very few women could even read. In fact, by no means every man could read, because many could not afford to pay a teacher, but most families tried to educate their sons if possible.

> **Crops**
> Most people think of rice as the most important food in China, and in the south that is true, but it is impossible to grow rice in most of the cold, dry North, and wheat and millet are the main crops there.

Sometimes, if a family was really poor, it would kill its newly born daughters, but it was rare to kill a son in this way. Here, about 80 years ago, a British missionary looks in a basket to see if any girl babies have been put in it instead of being drowned in the pond below.

Chinese Writing

Chinese word-pictures (characters) have changed from real pictures to being just bare-bones pictures, rather as we draw stick-men instead of taking the trouble to draw them like actual people. Here are some words showing the original pictures on the left and the modern characters on the right:

sheep

fish

eye

hand

rain

mountain

to stand

Other characters did not start out as pictures, but are just shapes which stand for ideas in the same way as the picture characters do. Here are some non-picture characters. It is easy to tell them apart from each other and from the picture-characters on the left.

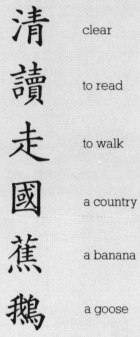

clear

to read

to walk

a country

a banana

a goose

There is no limit to the number of characters which can be thought up and new ones are still being invented to cope with new ideas and discoveries. Not surprisingly, Chinese dictionaries are very complicated to use.

Learning to read and write was a very difficult job and took a long while. The Chinese writing system does not "spell" words as English does. Instead it draws a symbol which stands for a word. English uses "s", "h", "e", "e" and "p" (sh-ee-p) to spell the sound of the word "sheep", but the Chinese word for sheep is a picture of a sheep's head with horns, 羊. Not all the symbols are pictures, but all of them are clearly different from each other. While it takes only 26 letters to write English there are as many Chinese characters as there are words to be written. To learn enough just to read and write with (about 3500 of them) is hard grind.

Anyone who has learned the alphabet can pronounce the word spelled s-h-e-e-p, but Chinese characters don't tell you how they should be pronounced. The character 羊 can be understood even if you don't know how to say it.

This means that Chinese characters could be used to write any language at all – all you would have to do is to say the word in the language of your choice. So 羊 could be pronounced "sheep" if you are an English-speaker, "mouton" if you are French, "schaf" if you are German, or "yang" if you come from Beijing in the north of China.

The language which people speak in China differs from area to area. There are seven major Chinese languages and many, many dialects of each of them. The languages and dialects are often very different from each other, and people from one part of the country cannot understand people from another part. It is rather like the situation in Europe, where there are lots of different languages.

In the south of China there is a large number of different types of Chinese spoken. This is probably the result of so many different groups of

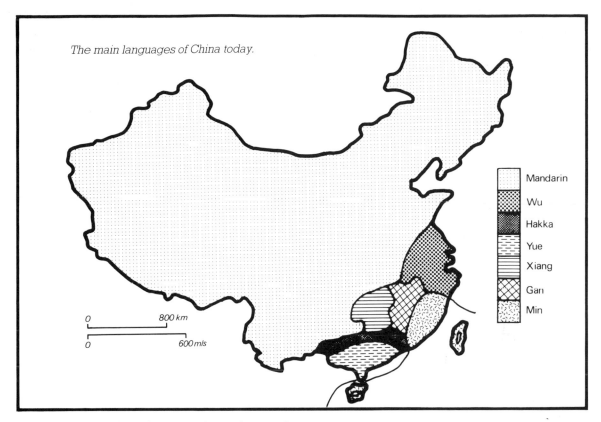

The main languages of China today.

- Mandarin
- Wu
- Hakka
- Yue
- Xiang
- Gan
- Min

0 — 800 km
0 — 600 mls

people coming into the area from the north. Chinese people feel happiest when talking to people in their own dialect. When they meet people from other dialect groups they feel uneasy and unfriendly and sometimes don't get on with each other very well.

Luckily for China the same written words can be used by everyone whatever the language they speak. A person in Beijing says "yang" for "sheep", someone in Hong Kong says "yeung", and a hundred miles along the coast they say "yeeay", but they all write 羊 and so can understand each other.

It is clear from what we have said so far that there were three important loyalties for a Chinese. First there was his family. It was always the family who were to be considered before others. If help was wanted – ask the family. If money was needed – ask the family. If he wanted to find a business partner – ask someone from the family. A man felt he could trust his family when he could not trust anyone else. In many ways this was an admirable thing. It gave a nice feeling of security and support: "all for one, one for all". In other ways it was not so good. It meant that a businessman would feel he had to employ a person just because he was a family member, not because he was the best person for the job (he might be completely useless). And a government

These two large characters read "Universal love". They were written by Dr Sun Yat-sen, the founder of the Republic of China. The written word is "universal" in China, because everyone reads and writes the same, regardless of which Chinese language they speak.

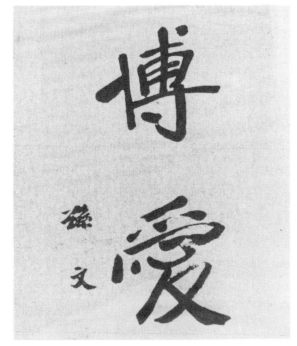

official would give special treatment to his relatives in a way which was unfair to the rest of the people.

The second loyalty was to a man's local area – his neighbours, village, town and local countryside. That is, a person felt that he belonged next after his family to the other people who spoke his dialect of Chinese.

The third loyalty was to those who were eligible to write and read Chinese. That is, to everyone else who was Chinese – people who spoke other dialects, the Emperor, the government, China.

All three loyalties were backed up by religions. The religion of the family was ancestor-worship. Chinese people believed that when a person died he or she became a god. This god would look after the living family members provided that they prayed properly and regularly. The family worshipped its ancestors every day. No one from outside the family could worship, so it was a very exclusive religion.

The religion of the local area was the worship of gods which were thought to protect the land and the people who lived on it. These gods looked after their own special territory, such as a village and its lands or a city and the countryside which was under its control. There were also some gods who had been real local people: they had been so good in their lifetime that everyone assumed they

Ancestor-worship

The ancestor's spirit is thought to be present in a tablet with his or her name on it. The tablet is kept in the home and the family offer incense and tea every day. On special occasions, such as weddings and festivals, all kinds of food, tea and wine are put before the ancestor as offerings. The ancestor is also present at the grave, and this spirit is visited and worshipped once or twice a year.

Old men kowtow (knock the head on the ground) to their ancestors at a ceremony in Hong Kong, South China.

Women making offerings of candles and incense at the funeral of a friend. A lot of importance was attached to death because this was the time when a living person became an ancestor-god.

One of the Kings of Hell. This paper god belonged to a small town which paraded it round "to catch ghosts" and return them to Hell where they belonged.

A local god (about 50cm high) who looked after the people who lived in a small lane. They reported all births, marriages and deaths to him, so that he acted like a kind of "heavenly registry office".

The Temple of Heaven in Beijing. Only the Emperor could worship here. Now it is a public park.

would continue to look after other people when they were dead.

The third loyalty had a religion as well. This state religion was practised by the Emperor and government officials, who worshipped on behalf of everyone in the country. The Emperor was the only person who was allowed to worship the highest god of all, the god who was called "Supreme Emperor" or just "Heaven".

Life for most people consisted of careful

farming throughout the year, with a few festivals to break the monotony. The most important of these festivals was New Year, when family members feasted, counted their blessings and prayed to all the gods for happiness and plenty in the year to come. Everyone added a year to his age at New Year, not on his birthday.

For most people then, it was a settled, stable life. The teachings of Confucius and other great Chinese thinkers encouraged people to be conservative and to find peace and enjoyment in the quiet country life and the warmth of the family home. There were traditionally four classes of people – scholars, farmers, craftsmen and merchants – and scholars and farmers were thought to be more important than the others.

Alas, there were always some people who were too poor to own land, or who were unable to find work, or who found it easier to turn to crime, or who were forced into illegal acts, or who gave up the struggle and became beggars. And, of course, there were the people who lived in cities, and obviously had to live a life which was different from that of the countryfolk.

New Year

The Chinese use two calendars, one a solar calendar like that used in the West, the other a lunar calendar. The lunar month runs from new moon to new moon, and all months are either 29 or 30 days long. The beginning of the first lunar month of the year is the New Year festival.

The moon and the sun have different cycles, and so the lunar months do not fit exactly into the solar year. Some lunar years have 12 months and some 13, and that way the lunar and solar calendars keep more or less in step. This is why the Chinese Lunar New Year festival falls at different times of the solar year, sometimes in early January, sometimes almost as late as March.

A page from the Chinese almanac. It covers the period 1-13 May 1967 and tells us that in the lunar calendar this was from the twenty-second day of the third moon to the fifth day of the fourth moon. It records an eclipse of the sun on 9 May.

4 Off the Bottom

The Han Chinese have always been proud of their country and their culture. Looking about them they could see other countries and peoples who admired China so much that they copied her.

Over a thousand years ago the Japanese began to use the Chinese writing system, to model their cities on Chinese cities, to copy the Chinese practice of ancestor-worship, and so on. The Koreans and the Vietnamese did much the same. Although China was conquered several times by foreign armies, the invaders always ended up by adopting a Chinese way of life.

The message in all this was quite clear to Chinese people: "China (and everything which is Chinese) is superior to everywhere else." It did not make sense to want to leave China – why go to somewhere which was, by definition, not so good? For the same reason the Chinese have seldom shown any desire to conquer territory beyond their own natural land borders.

But China has not been able to ignore other countries completely because there was always the possibility of attack from abroad.

By the fourteenth century she had a policy of trying to form a ring of "buffer states" around the country. These states were to be self-governing but friendly to China. The "tribute system" was the means of carrying out the policy. The buffer states acknowledged China's superiority by sending gifts (tribute) to the Emperor at regular intervals. Often the presents the Emperor gave in return were even more valuable than the tribute. It was the act of homage which was important to China, not the value of the tribute gifts. Among the countries which paid regular tribute were Korea (annually), Annam (Vietnam) (every two years), Siam (Thailand) (every three years), Burma and Laos (every ten years).

In the Ming dynasty the desire to bring more and more countries into this tribute system seemed to grow strong. The Emperor began to send great fleets out to the islands of South-East Asia and the Indian Ocean. In A.D. 1405 the first of a series of major voyages by the admiral Zheng He (Cheng Ho) took place. The fleets of "treasure

---

Ming Dynasty Voyages
Even in the twentieth century we can be impressed with the size of the fleets:

> These embassies must have been stupendous undertakings; fleets are described of 62 vessels carrying 37,000 soldiers; more than 20 countries in the Indian archipelago [group of islands] and the Indian Ocean were visited; chiefs and kings, like those of Palembang and of Ceylon, were deposed and sent as captives to China, and members of the expeditions went as far as Aden and Mecca, bringing messages from the Chinese court.

(J.J.L. Duyvendak, *Ma Huan Re-Examined*, Amsterdam, 1933)

---

ships" went all over South-East Asia; to Ceylon and India, to the Persian Gulf, to the Red Sea and the coast of East Africa. In the more distant places the fleet was merely "showing the flag", exploring, looking for exotic goods and making diplomatic contacts. But in South-East Asia local rulers were asked to promise loyalty to the Chinese emperor, and even if they did not have to send tribute they were felt to be afraid enough of China's might that they would never be a threat to her.

The last of the voyages began in 1431 and ended in 1433, and after that China seems to have lost interest in the area. Chinese governments turned their attention anxiously towards the north, where, as always, there was the threat of invasion. But although the government turned away from the "Southern Ocean", as it is called in Chinese, the people did not. There had been some Chinese traders operating there even before Zheng He's voyages, and their numbers began to increase afterwards. This did not please the government. In the traditional division of people into four classes, traders were the lowest of all,

A later ship "showing the flag". This is the junk Keying *visiting London in 1847.*

and to have such low-class representatives going abroad was felt to be quite wrong for the most important country on earth. Besides, as we have seen, it was hard for them to understand why anyone should want to leave China at all. The Emperors began to pass laws aimed at stopping movement out of China.

It was not just traders who ventured abroad: other Chinese were going too. In A.D. 1712 the Emperor announced that anyone who left China and tried to remain abroad should be sent back by the government of the country he was in and immediately beheaded. A few years later, in 1717, the same Emperor relented and pardoned all those who came back to China, but he still forbad others to leave the country. A later Emperor tried to stop the movement by passing severe sentences on the people who were running the travel businesses which booked the sea passages. Right up until 1893 it was illegal to leave China except with special permission from the Emperor.

None of these laws seems to have had much effect on the situation. People ignored the laws and managed to escape from the coastguards. As the years went by, the trickle of emigrants

Anti-Emigration Law
Here is a translation of part of the Chinese law on emigration which was in force in 1799:

> All officers of government, soldiers, and private citizens, who clandestinely [secretly] proceed to sea to trade, or who remove to foreign islands for the purpose of inhabiting and cultivating the same, shall be punished according to the law against communicating with rebels and enemies, and consequently suffer death by being beheaded. The governors of cities of the second and third orders, shall like-wise be beheaded when found guilty of combining with, or artfully conniving at [encouraging] the conduct of such persons.
>
> (Sir George Staunton, *Ta Tsing Leu Lee: being the fundamental laws, and a selection from the supplementary statutes, of the Penal Code of China*, London, 1810, pp. 543-4)

became a stream and then, in the second half of the nineteenth century, a flood. Between 1840 and 1900 the number of people who left China for

A Chinese war junk in 1857.

other countries was probably well over two million.

The Chinese government said that no-one should leave the country, and the Chinese people themselves believed that it was better to live in China, so how could all this have happened?

First, the population of China had been growing very fast. By 1741 there were over 143 million people in China and by 1850, after long years of peace and prosperity, nearly 430 million. China was able to begin feeding more people because of improvements in the kinds of rice that were being grown and because of the introduction of new crops from elsewhere. Particularly important was the arrival from America of maize, potatoes, sweet potatoes and peanuts. These crops could be grown in places where traditional crops did badly, so that more land was made useful. But once the population had started to grow it went on growing, and by the nineteenth century there was often not enough food to go round. Hungry people left their homes to look for land to farm and food to eat. Many of them, of course, moved southwards towards the coast.

Second, the middle of the nineteenth century marked the end of a period of peace and good government in China. In 1850 a huge and very bloody rebellion broke out in the south-west of the country. The rebel leader, Hong Xiuquan, wanted to overthrow the Emperor and set up a "Heavenly Kingdom of Peace" with himself as king. It took 14 years for the rebels to be defeated, and by then more than 20 million people had been killed. This civil war left cities and towns almost empty and some of the best land in China was ruined. Refugees from the war (and from other rebellions which followed it) fled southwards.

Third, it was possible to make a good living, and perhaps even to get very rich, in the lands overseas. People were attracted by the chance of making money and coming back to China to retire in luxury.

Fourth, the nineteenth and early twentieth centuries were times when Western nations were ruling large empires throughout the world. Many of the colonies were short of labour and encouraged people from other countries to move to work for them. After 1842 a number of ports began to open on the south coast of China and Western ships could sail in to pick up passengers and take them to the colonies and countries which needed them. It was quite easy for anyone who wanted to leave the country to get a passage on a foreign ship, which the Chinese coastguards would at that time not dare to stop and search. The most important ports for emigration were

Treaty ports

In 1839 all the opium in the possession of the British merchants in China was seized and destroyed by the Chinese official whose job it was to stamp out the evil of opium smoking. We would now see this as a splendid action, but at the time the British merchants bitterly resented it, and they managed to persuade the government in London to send out troops to make China pay for daring to interfere with "trade". In the Opium War which followed, the British forced the Chinese to surrender and to sign the Treaty of Nanking in 1842. One of the terms of the treaty was that five ports should be opened for trade with foreign nations. After a second war, another treaty was signed in 1860 which opened 11 more ports. These 16 ports, and others which were opened later, were known as Treaty Ports. Trade with China became much busier and easier because of them.

Amoy, Guangzhou (Canton), Hong Kong, Macau and Swatow.

There were different reasons why a Chinese should go abroad despite the government ban. One man might do it to get rich, another to escape from the clutches of the law, another because he was too hungry to refuse the temptation of being fed on the ship, another because he wanted to do a different kind of job. All these reasons and others were really part of the same thing: China had become full up with people and the pressure of the huge population pushing southwards, as usual, was forcing some people to "fall off the bottom of the map".

Most of those who fell off the bottom were poor, landless, and badly educated or illiterate. They were men (only a few women emigrated) who were "losers", men who could not cope well in China. Not promising material at all, and they could not look to any Chinese government help if they got into trouble abroad. When a high official was asked in 1858 to appoint consuls to look after the tens of thousands of Chinese who had gone to

South China coastal ports which handled the migrant traffic.

Trouble with the law: laws were very harsh by the standards of British law. One of the punishments was to walk around with the heavy wooden cangue *locked over the shoulders. This is a Western artist's impression from the late nineteenth century.*

the United States in the Californian gold-rush, he replied:

> It is not our custom to send officials beyond our borders. When the Emperor rules over so many millions, what does he care for the few waifs that have drifted away to a foreign land? The Emperor's wealth is beyond computation.

Why should he care for those of his subjects who have left their home, or for the sands they have scraped together?

(W.A.P. Martin, *Cycle of Cathay: or China South and North, with Personal Reminiscences*, New York, 1896, p. 160)

We shall see later how well these "waifs" fared.

5 How They Went

Some of the earliest travellers from China may have gone by land routes to the countries of mainland South-East Asia, that is, to Siam (Thailand), Annam (Vietnam), Burma, and so on. But most of the contact with mainland as well as island South-East Asia has been by sea.

We know that Chinese Buddhist pilgrims sailed to Indonesia and India from the fifth to the eighth centuries, so by then there must have been Chinese ships big enough and strong enough to sail the high seas. Afterwards, the Arabs took over most of the shipping trade, but by the twelfth century Chinese ships were again busy in the area. Their journeys were made safer and easier by the use of the magnetic compass. A hundred years before Europeans discovered it the Chinese were steering with the aid of the compass, making journeys out of sight of land much less dangerous.

Unfortunately, we do not have any good descriptions of these early ships, but we know from Marco Polo's account, written in A.D. 1298,

Even within sight of land, voyaging could be dangerous. This map is from a Chinese book of 1819. It bears only the sketchiest relationship to the real coastline and islands and would be more hazardous than helpful to a sea captain.

Junks

Small Chinese boats which are rowed or sculled are often called *sampans*. The name comes from the Cantonese word *saam-baan* meaning "three planks", which describes quite clearly their small size. Larger boats and ocean-going traditional Chinese sailing ships are known as *junks*. This word is a mispronunciation of the Chinese word *chuan*, which means quite simply "ship". Now there are even "motorized junks", which look much like the old ships but have engines.

Junks and a sampan in the late nineteenth century.

that they had watertight compartments, which European ships did not have until nearly 600 years later. The ships were built of fir timber, with four masts, and had 50 or 60 cabins. They had crews of 200 or 300 men. Probably they were very much like the great sea-going junks of South China which could still be seen in quite recent times. A nineteenth-century writer, talking about the peculiar ships which could be seen in Singapore harbour, says:

> Most peculiar and most striking of all are the huge Chinese junks, some of 600 or 700 tons measurement, which during the greater part

of the year lie anchored there. Though the largest of these junks must measure quite as much as I state, yet the great majority are much smaller; but it is singular that in shape and generally in rig, all are nearly similar. Indeed, the very sampans, or two-oared China boats, used to convey native passengers and luggage to and from the ships and the shore, are identical in shape. All have alike the square bow and the broad flat stern; and, from the largest to the smallest, on what in a British vessel would be called her "head boards", all have the two eyes embossed and painted. John Chinaman's explanation of this custom, according to general account, "no got eyes, no can see", is but little complimentary to the good sense of his utilitarian and sensible nation.

(John Cameron, *Our Tropical Possessions in Malayan India*, London, 1865, p. 39)

When the great flood of emigrants began in the nineteenth century it was in junks that they faced the dangers of the ocean. Different ports preferred different colours for their junks, Amoy liking green, other places using black or yellow, and Swatow junks being painted with red varnish. An old man who remembered back to the 1880s told how,

. . . when I was a boy, our village had eight sea-going junks. On their voyages north they

Pidgin English

Pidgin was a strange language which was a mixture of English and Chinese. It was used between Chinese and foreign people as a business language which both could handle. "Pidgin" was the word they used meaning "business". "No got eyes no can see" is Pidgin for "It cannot see without eyes". We use a few Pidgin words in ordinary English today. "To have a look-see" and "Long time no see" are two common examples.

Neither the Westerners nor the Chinese were very polite about each other. To call someone a "Chinaman", or "John Chinaman" was not as polite as "a Chinese". And many Chinese talked of "red-haired devils" or "barbarian devils" instead of "Westerners".

"No got eyes no can see". A small cargo launch on the Singapore River (bottom left) still had "eyes" painted on the bow in the 1970s.

"1000 Mile Eyes" is worshipped by sailors along the coast of China. They believe he will help them to spot danger in good time to escape from it.

"1000 Mile Eyes" is worshipped by sailors along the coast of China. They believe he will help them to spot danger in good time to escape from it.

misery on the junk, so perhaps he was a paying passenger who had good treatment. It was not so comfortable for many of the people who travelled.

The demand for overseas workers grew, and more and more people began to get involved in the movement abroad. Conditions on board the junks became worse, crowded and unhealthy. The passengers were often tricked into going by unscrupulous agents who told them that they would be rich in no time. A British colonial official reported in 1877:

> "Look how poor you are," Lew Ship Yit complained that a recruiter had said to him; "If you follow me I can take you to Singapore, where you will get such good employment that very soon you will pay the small amount of

would often call at Shanghai and Tientsin, and carry cargoes of Swatow oranges and sugar cane. On their southward voyages they usually went to Bangkok, carrying beans, tea, and silk as their major cargoes. The largest junk carried over two hundred passengers. Usually a passenger took with him a water jar of local pottery, two suits of summer clothes, a round straw hat, and a straw mat. The voyage from Swatow to Bangkok often took a month. After setting foot on the junk, while waiting for it to sail, we could do little but trust Heaven as to our safety during the voyage.

(Ta Chen, *Emigrant Communities in South China*, London, 1939, p. 261)

The old man says nothing about discomfort or

A Crowded, Nightmare Voyage
The journeys were not just uncomfortable, they often caused the death of passengers:

> By their death, though there may be a loss of profit, there can be none of capital to the shipper. The men cost nothing and the more the shipper can cram into his vessel the greater must be his profit. It would be a better speculation for the trader whose junk could only carry properly 300 men, to take on board 600 – and lose 250 – on the way down, than it would be for him to start with his legitimate number and land them all safely; for, in the first case, he would bring 350 men to market, and, in the other, only 300.

(John Cameron, *Our Tropical Possessions in Malayan India*, London, 1865, pp. 42-3)

In 1874 the Straits Settlements laid down the maximum number of passengers which any ship could carry, but afterwards there were still reports of overloaded vessels being met outside the harbour by smaller junks which took off the extra passengers before the authorities could count them.

passage money required and will save more than $50-60 a year."

(*Proceedings of Legislative Council, Straits Settlements*, 1877)

Alas, conditions in Singapore were not quite as rosy as the recruiters promised. It often took a whole year for a man to work off the cost of his fare, and wages were not always as good as they were said to be.

Some passengers were able to pay their fares in advance, but many were too poor to do so. They had to go "on credit", and that meant that they were more or less prisoners from the moment they agreed to go. The agent in China was paid by results, so he wanted to make sure that they got on the boat. He would have them shut up in a boarding-house till it was ready to sail. After a crowded, nightmare voyage the passengers were kept shut up below deck until the receiving agent or employer paid the fare and agent's fee. And even then the migrants were treated like prisoners until they had worked long enough to pay back the money their employer had spent on them. The Chinese called this trade in human lives "selling pigs": it is not hard to see why.

Even these poor men were better off than some, because they had at least agreed to be "pigs". But other men were kidnapped and shipped off abroad by force. In 1864 the situation had become so bad in Guangdong Province that the governor-general wrote to the Emperor to ask for the death penalty to be passed on anyone who kidnapped and sold people overseas. The Emperor agreed.

In 1874 a commission of enquiry in Cuba was told that four out of every five Chinese on the island had been sent there by kidnappers or swindlers who had not told them where they were going. More than one person in ten had died on the ships on the way, some from illness, some from ill-treatment, and some by committing suicide.

It was not only on Chinese sailing junks that there were poor conditions. When the migrants travelled on Western-owned ships conditions could be terrible:

Many of the vessels which left Chinese ports between 1845 and 1875 were simply slavers. In 1872 it was officially denied from Hong Kong that any undue restriction was placed on coolie passengers there. Some months previously, the *Don Juan* had left Macao with 640 coolies on board. In mid-ocean she took fire, and the captain and crew abandoned her. Only a few coolies were on deck, and they were mostly in chains. The iron gratings on the hatches were locked, and the keys were not to be found. When the wretched crowd below burst open the fore-hatch, it was too late, and all but fifty perished.

(W.P. Reeves, in P.C. Campbell, *Chinese Coolie Emigration*, London, 1923, p. xiii)

By the turn of the century attempts were being made in China and abroad to stop the worst of the

---

Death at Sea

Diseases which killed the emigrants on board ship included dysentery, scurvy, cholera, typhus, yellow fever and typhoid. Overcrowding, lack of fresh air, rotten food and bad water made them easy victims to disease. Suicide by jumping overboard was one way out of misery, but ships' crews did their best to stop their "pigs" from being lost like this: those who were allowed on deck were often chained up. Fires were common, some of them started by the emigrants themselves when they "mutinied" against bad treatment.

The *Norway*, one of the largest American clippers, was bound from Macau to Havana with one thousand Chinese emigrants in 1859. On the fifth night out, the Chinese lighted joss paper and threatened to set the ship on fire. The mate rushed to the main hatch and blocked the door, then the stewards passed out to everyone blunderbusses, cutlasses, and pistols from the arms chest. Then tarpaulins were thrown over the forward hatches and a stream of water pumped on to them. This turned the flames into smoke and drove the Chinese aft to avoid suffocation. The fighting lasted two days. Exhausted after failing in every attempt, the Chinese quietly lay down and went to sleep. Seventy Chinese had either been killed or died of wounds during the struggle.

(Sing-Wu Wang, *The Organization of Chinese Emigration 1848-1888*, San Francisco, 1978, pp. 244-5)

abuses. In 1899 the Emperor announced that it was clear that there were now many Chinese working abroad and there was no reason to suppose that they were not loyal subjects of China. In future ambassadors and consuls should try to help and protect Chinese people in their districts.

In 1904, when workmen were urgently needed in South Africa for the gold mines there, the British and Chinese Governments worked out an agreement on how Chinese labourers should be hired and treated. The terms of the agreement were not favourable to the Chinese, but it was a move in the right direction.

During the First World War both the British and French Governments wanted to recruit extra manpower. After negotiations with the Chinese Government nearly 200,000 men went on contract to serve in France in the British and French labour corps. Conditions of service this time were much better supervised and the workers – officially called "coolies" in their contracts – were reasonably paid and looked after.

Very different conditions existed by the time of the most recent Chinese migration. After the Second World War, there were openings for restuarant work in Britain and Western Europe. The emigrant area this time was Hong Kong, and particularly the New Territories of Hong Kong. Here the effects of falling prices for rice and of population pressure were again to push people "off the bottom". From the mid-1950s onwards a growing stream of men left for Europe.

What was new was the decline of sea travel as airlines began to expand. Most of the new migrants travelled by air, reaching their destination quickly and in no more crowded conditions than any other air passenger. But

Coolies

The word "coolie" comes from the Chinese word *ku-li*, meaning "hard labour". Most of the men who migrated in the second half of the nineteenth century were employed in physical labour and the name was originally used because of this. *Ku* actually means 'bitter', and there is no doubt that many of the men had very bitter experiences.

Young coolies in the late nineteenth century.

regular fares were expensive, and soon special companies were set up to charter whole aircraft and so be able to sell cheaper tickets to the migrants. By 1970 one charter company was offering tickets at only about a third of the normal cost on a scheduled airline.

Air travel was certainly more comfortable than the old junk voyages, and it was much less risky. But it was not always fun:

> The agencies cannot always afford to reserve an airplane for a fixed date of departure, so most of the "Restaurant Workers' Specials" operate on a flexible schedule. Passengers have to be ready to leave on twelve hours' notice any time within a ten-day period. Sometimes the flights may be delayed three or four times and may actually leave a month later than expected. Although the workers and their employers have learned to accept these delays as inevitable, they still cause a great deal of concern and anguish among the emigrants.
>
> (James L. Watson, *Emigration and the Chinese Lineage*, University of California Press, 1975, pp. 91-2)

From junks to steamships to aircraft, the migrations went on. Conditions of travel, of work, of pay, and of housing improved over the years, but many of the ways of life of the Chinese abroad did not change.

One of the things most dear to the heart of the emigrants was the hope of returning home wealthy to their villages to retire in comfort. It has always been the case that a majority of those who went overseas went home again later. Perhaps as many as two-thirds returned home, though by no means all of them were rich.

Some men died before they could return to China, but there was a way of making their dreams of home come true after death. Their bodies would be sent back to their villages to be buried by their families in the only land which they valued – the hills and valleys of South China.

> It is well known that, no matter where they die, the bodies of overseas Chinese have, where possible, usually been conveyed back to their homes for burial. . . . Coffins and remains of Chinese who died in various parts of the world, e.g. Borneo, the Philippines, Indonesia, the U.S.A., have been shipped to China via Hong Kong which in prewar and immediately postwar days enjoyed a certain pre-eminence as a transit centre for the onward movement of human remains. . . . The accommodation ranges from single rooms, where one or more coffins rest on trestles, to larger rooms holding hundreds of coffins, together with exhumed remains in a variety of receptacles, e.g. earthenware urns, rattan baskets, wooden boxes and even secondhand tin containers.
>
> (B.D. Wilson, "Chinese Burial Customs in Hong Kong", *Journal of the Hong Kong Branch of the Royal Asiatic Society*, Vol. I, 1961, pp. 115-16)

An American who studied a village in Guangdong Province wrote in 1925:

> Once in a while a fortunate villager returns home with wealth and foreign wife, trailing a flock of queerly-dressed children. It is thus

---

Typhoon

In 1903 Joseph Conrad wrote a wonderfully exciting short story called *Typhoon* about a steamship taking Chinese men back to China. The ship was on her way "to the treaty port of Fu-chau, with some cargo in her lower holds, and two hundred Chinese coolies returning to their village homes in the province of Fo-kien, after a few years of work in various tropical colonies". She ran into a terrible typhoon which might easily have sunk her. The Chinese were locked in a hold and someone suggested that they change direction to avoid the storm and make the journey more comfortable for the passengers:

> "Passengers?" wondered the Captain gravely. "What passengers?"
> "Why, the Chinamen, sir", explained Jukes, very sick of this conversation.
> "The Chinamen! Why don't you speak plainly? Couldn't tell what you meant. Never heard a lot of coolies spoken of as passengers before. Passengers, indeed! What's come to you?"

Travel seems to have been no more pleasant on the way home than it was on the crowded ships going overseas from China.

A row of earthenware urns on a hillside in China. Each one contains the bones of one person. The urns will eventually be buried in a permanent grave nearby.

quite natural that a father blesses a departing son. In his emigrant kin he finds an additional source of income. But the sons of luck are few. The majority of the emigrants from Phenix village come back with empty hands, but richer through sad experience, or else in distant lands complete their journey to "West Heaven" [Paradise].

(D.H. Kulp, *Country Life in South China*, New York, 1925, p. 86)

However many Chinese went home, there were always some who stayed, and these formed the populations which still exist in countries all over the world. Many of them had been drawn overseas by the hope of making money in the colonies run by Western nations. Now almost all of the Western colonies and the Westerners have gone, but the Chinese stay on.

6 To Thailand

Siam, called Thailand since 1949, was one of the earliest countries to attract Chinese emigrants.

There were certainly some Chinese there 600 years ago, and the Thai kings first sent tribute to

Thailand.

China in A.D. 1296. The emigration started on quite a small scale and even 300 years later there were only about 3000 Chinese who had made their homes there. The strongest flow of emigrants did not come until the late nineteenth and early twentieth centuries. There are now probably about three million people of Chinese origin in Thailand, but many of the total population of nearly 50 million have some Chinese blood, as there has been a great deal of intermarriage with the Thais.

Some of the early Chinese visitors moved into the country overland from the south of Yunnan province, but most came by sea from the south coast of China. Their knowledge of the seas was very useful to the Thais:

> The Siamese kings used Chinese economic advisers and entrusted other natural resources to Chinese traders. The most important of these was timber with which the Chinese built up a flourishing ship-building industry. This was a most significant development. Chinese sailors manned most of the junks built in Siam and the Chinese soon controlled both the coastal and inland river transport of the country. It is well to remember that many of the Chinese junks sailing the Nanyang [Southern Ocean] during this period were either owned by or on contract to the Siamese kings and that in the eighteenth century Siam was the most important centre of Nanyang Chinese activity.

(Wang Gungwu, *A Short History of the Nanyang Chinese*, Singapore, 1959, p. 16)

Western visitors to Siam were not very impressed with Chinese seamanship. A Jesuit missionary, Father Tachard, writing in 1687 about Chinese junks there, said: "though that nation brag that they have had the use of the compass for above two thousand years, yet they come very far short of the European in the art of navigation." And the famous Protestant missionary, Charles Gutzlaff, who was in Siam in 1831, wrote:

> The navigation of junks is performed without the aid of charts, or any other helps, except the compass; it is mere coasting, and the whole art of the pilot consists in directing the course

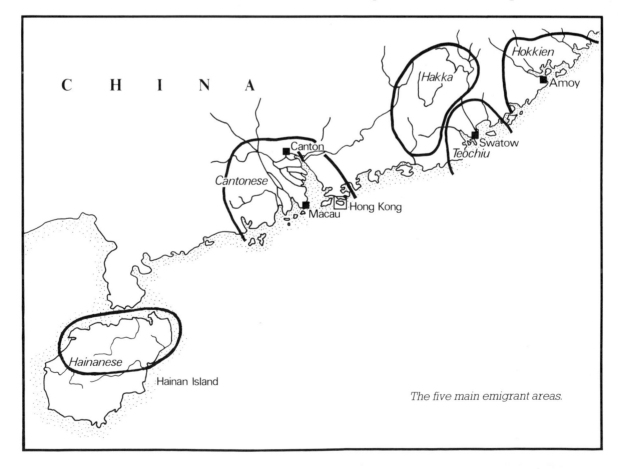

The five main emigrant areas.

A Hainanese junk running before the wind.

according to the promontories in sight. In time of danger, the men immediately lose all their courage; and their indecision frequently proves the destruction of their vessel. . . .

The Chinese sailors are, generally, from the most debased class of people. The major part of them are opium-smokers, gamblers, thieves, and fornicators. . . . They are poor and in debt; they cheat, and are cheated by one another, whenever it is possible.

(Charles Gutzlaff, *Journal of Three Voyages along the Coast of China*, London, 1834, pp. 57 and 61)

Whatever the Westerners thought of the Chinese seamen, the fact is that for centuries they were of great importance to Thailand, and it was in their ships that many of the Chinese immigrants travelled.

The Chinese in Thailand came from five different areas of China. The Hainanese people from Hainan island had the shortest distance to travel. Next closest were the Cantonese people from the Pearl River delta area. The Teochiu (or Swatow or Chaozhou) were from higher up the coast, the Hakka from just inland of them, and the Hokkien were the farthest away, opposite the large island of Taiwan. All these people spoke different Chinese languages and had different ways of life.

When they arrived in Thailand these groups tended to go into different jobs. The Hainanese (sometimes called "Hailam" people) were mostly in the poorest-paid work. They became servants, waiters, market gardeners, fishermen, miners and manual labourers. In fact, they were typical "coolies", working hard for other people.

The Teochiu were the largest group of migrants and they could be found in all kinds of jobs. The wealthiest and most important businessmen were mostly Teochiu, and they were very much in control of the rice trade, which was responsible for much of Thailand's wealth. But some Teochiu, such as the dock workers and the transport labourers, were in poorly paid jobs.

Many Hokkien people also became wealthy merchants, and they were particularly important in the tea trade. But Hokkien could be found in coolie-type jobs as well, especially in the tin mines of south Thailand.

The Cantonese ran the building businesses and skilled trades such as engineering and carpentry. Poorer Cantonese were employed in the building trade as labourers.

Hakka, like Hainanese, were generally unable to get into higher-paid work. They became small tradesmen and shopkeepers, leatherworkers, tailors and hairdressers. Quite a lot of Hakka were in coolie jobs.

Of course, none of this happened overnight. Almost all the Chinese who came to Thailand came with little more than the clothes they stood up in. They did not become rice-mill owners or building contractors or shopkeepers straight away, but slowly worked their way up. Those who were poor could always see plenty of examples of others who had been just as poor before they made their money, and this was an encouragement to them to do the same.

How could the Chinese make good in competition with the Thais themselves? The answer seems to be that there was not a great deal of competition. The Thai lived in a land where it was not necessary to work very hard to get a satisfactory living. The climate was good

A Success Story
Zhang Ding was a Teochiu who went to Bangkok in the 1870s. He arrived owing the money for his passage:

> He worked first as a cook, then as a rice-polishing "coolie". Next he began operating a sampan ferry across the river at Bangkok, earning three baht a month, after which he became a market gardener making ten baht. Soon he had enough savings to lend money to those even poorer than himself, thus increasing his capital until in 1882 he established a small export business of his own. By this time he was sufficiently affluent to marry into a good family in North Siam, and his mother-in-law, who was friendly with the governor of Lampang, obtained for him an excellent teak forest concession. While the firm expanded, he became a subfarmer of three gambling houses and a spirit-farm operator. By the first decade of the twentieth century, his company owned five rice mills, a sawmill and a dockyard.
> (G.W. Skinner, *Chinese Society in Thailand: an Analytical History*, New York, 1957, p. 137)

and the soil was fertile. With not too much effort the people could grow quite enough to feed themselves and they did not feel the need to do much more than that.

The Chinese, on the other hand, came from a land where they had to work hard for even a basic living standard. They were used to the idea of hard work and of ambition to create wealth.

Success didn't come overnight. A lowly dish-mender gets a customer.

Poisoning Chinese Men

It used to be said that when Chinese husbands went back to China to visit their families there they were given a slow-acting poison by their Thai wives. If they didn't return within a year the poison would take effect and they would die, because only the Thai wife knew the cure. Whether the men believed this, or whether they only told their Chinese families to make sure that there would be no fuss about going back to Thailand, is hard to say. Certainly some of the families in China believed it to be true.

When they got to Thailand they found that the Thais were already farming but were not strong in business skills or manufacturing. So the Chinese could do jobs which did not compete with the Thais and which paid very well.

Before 1920 almost all the Chinese who went abroad were men. Some of them were married, but they left their wives and families behind. In Thailand they met Thai girls and married them. Even those men with wives already in China took Thai wives because, until the 1950s, there was nothing wrong to a Chinese in having more than one wife. Since there is little physical difference between the Thais and the Chinese, their children, or at least their grandchildren, would be hard to tell apart from ordinary Thai people. There was not much ill-will or racial prejudice caused by the intermarriage.

Gutzlaff, the missionary, not a sympathetic man to the Chinese (or to the Thais for that matter), wrote in 1834:

> They delight to live in wretchedness and filth, and are very anxious to conform to the vile habits of the Siamese. In some cases when they enter into matrimonial alliances with these latter, they even throw away their jackets and trousers, and become Siamese in their very dress . . . within two or three generations, all the distinguishing marks of the Chinese character dwindle entirely away; and a nation which adheres so obstinately to its national customs becomes wholly changed to Siamese.
>
> (Charles Gutzlaff, *Journal of Three Voyages along the Coast of China*, London, 1934 pp. 34-5)

Until the twentieth century there was very little antagonism towards the Chinese. In fact, a large majority of the population had some Chinese blood in its veins. Where there was a clear difference in dress, language, customs and behaviour it was because of the continued arrival of new Chinese migrants.

But, from the beginning of this century, Chinese women and whole families started to emigrate to Thailand. This soon changed the ideas of the Chinese men about marriage. Instead of marrying Thai wives, they took Chinese brides. But that meant that they didn't have Thai relations any more, and Thai relations had always been important in helping the Chinese to work without problems.

Also, now that the Chinese only married other Chinese they could be easily told apart from the Thais, and there began to be racial prejudice problems. By the 1940s laws were being passed to stop the Chinese from working in certain trades. These included making, casting or selling images of the Buddha; making women's hats; cutting or tailoring women's dresses; making fireworks, dolls and toys; hair waving and cutting;

This Chinese street barber would have been unable to earn his living in Thailand after 1942.

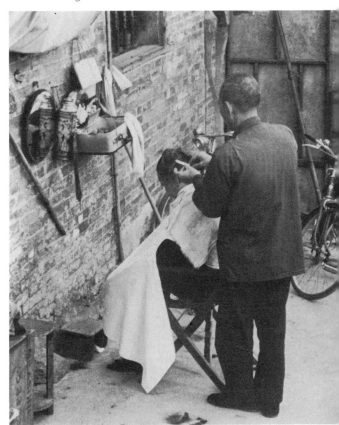

legal work. Schools which had been set up to teach Chinese children in Chinese were closed down. The Thai government did its best to stop many Chinese immigrants coming into the country, and those that did come in were heavily taxed.

In spite of all these restrictions the Chinese have managed to make a good living in Thailand. They are still in control of the rice market and have important positions in other industries and trades.

What was life like for a Chinese immigrant to Thailand? Here is a life story fairly typical of a successful nineteenth-century migrant. We will call him Wang Wuming.

Wang was born near Swatow in a poor village which suffered constantly from famine. It was often flooded, and yellow lines could be seen on the walls of the houses where the floodwaters reached. In 1858, when he was 15, Wang set out on a junk for Thailand. He took only the clothes he stood up in and a bamboo carrying-pole. By the time he arrived in Bangkok every cent he had had been spent on his fare and food.

At Bangkok he went straight to the home of an uncle from his village and there he was given some space in a room, a rattan sleeping-mat and a little money to buy goods with and set up as a pedlar. Next morning he got up and went out to earn his living.

The Pigtail

Sometimes called a "queue", the pigtail was the hair-style worn by all Chinese men from the mid-seventeenth century up to this century. When China was conquered by the Manchu people in 1644 they made the Chinese wear their hair this way to show their submission. Chinese who went abroad did not cut it off because most of them wanted to go back to China and they would have risked execution as revolutionaries if they had no pigtail when they got there. It was only when the Manchu (Qing) dynasty was overthrown in 1912 that it was possible to cut off the pigtail.

Playing a trick on pigtailed men. A late nineteenth-century drawing of a practical joke.

He was a thin, dark-faced boy, dressed in a faded blue loose jacket and blue trousers rolled up to his knees. His legs were sturdy, and his bare feet were turned outwards as they slapped on the hot roads. He had a length of cloth round his neck as a sweatrag. The hair on the front of his head was shaved bare, but at the back it had never been cut and hung down nearly to his waist in a long, plaited pigtail.

On his right shoulder he balanced his bamboo pole and from each end hung baskets in which he put whatever he had to sell that day. This work did not bring in much money, but his uncle saw that he was hard-working and honest and that he did not waste his money and his health on opium smoking as lots of other men did.

A Chinese merchant in Thailand in 1900. Both men and women used fans, and the large umbrella would have been made of oiled paper rather than fabric. Umbrellas doubled up as sunshades.

One day he took Wang to meet a rich rice merchant who came from the same area near Swatow. The merchant gave Wang a job as a rice-coolie, carrying loads of rice around, and soon afterwards he promoted him to be in charge of a whole team of coolies.

Now he was earning enough money to send some back to his parents in China and even to pay back his uncle for the food and lodging he had so kindly been given when he arrived in Bangkok. Before long he was lending money to other Chinese and taking interest on it when it was returned. Then he used all his savings to buy some timber and rice, which he put on a junk going back to Swatow. It was a very successful deal and he made a considerable profit.

By the time he was 25 he was doing very well. He married a Thai wife and set her up in business as a storekeeper. Between them they prospered and she introduced Wang to many of her Thai relations and friends who helped him to get important business contracts.

At the age of 58, now a very wealthy rice-mill owner, he left his wife and children to carry on the business while he went back to his old village in China. There he died three years later. In 1904 his eldest son (who had no pigtail) gave a large sum of money to the Bangkok Tian Hua Hospital as a memorial to his name.

Of course, not all migrants to Thailand were as successful as Wang Wuming. Some men did not work as hard as he did. Others were unlucky in business. Others were opium smokers or gamblers or spendthrifts who squandered all the money they earned. Over the years, there were many who died penniless and were cremated at the expense of charitable men from their own speech group. According to one writer, in a village near Swatow,

> . . . not more than one-tenth of the emigrants return successful. Many of them, while in foreign lands, are barely able to send back enough money to keep their families alive. Not a few persons are forced to live from hand to mouth, finally returning broken in productive efficiency, a charge upon their families, or dying miserable deaths away from home with none to burn the candles.

(D.H. Kulp, *Country Life in South China*, New York, 1925, p. 53)

Clubhouses for speech group associations. These are on a quiet island in Hong Kong.

In Chapter Three we saw that there were three loyalties which were important to the Chinese. Of the three, the one which seems to have meant most to the Chinese in Thailand was the loyalty to local area.

Each of the five speech groups (Teochiu, Hokkien, Hakka, Hainanese and Cantonese) formed a separate association or club. These associations founded schools which taught in their own language, and they also ran cemeteries, and hospitals. Their offices were social centres where anyone from that speech group could go for a chat, or to play mahjong, or for advice on sending money back to China, or for help with finding a job or loan, or for settling arguments. The associations at one time also built temples so that their members would have somewhere to worship.

The other loyalties were for many years not so much a part of the migrants' lives. Until this century almost all the wives of Chinese men in Thailand were Thai. These Thai women had considerable influence over their children, with the result that they often grew up more Thai than

Chinese. In other words, they never had a Chinese family background to which to be loyal. In the same way, a lot of the children born to these mixed marriages did not have enough contact with Chinese culture to want to be loyal to it.

Once Chinese women started to emigrate to Thailand the situation changed and the three loyalties all began to count. It was then that the Thais felt threatened and passed laws to try to stop Chinese control of their economy.

So what is the difference now between a Chinese and a Thai? No one can easily answer that question. Almost everyone in Thailand has some Chinese blood, but that is not enough to make them Chinese. Those who do not take Thai names but continue to use Chinese names are probably showing that they want to be thought of as Chinese. Those who belong to Chinese speech group associations or who have only Chinese blood are certainly Chinese. There are quite enough Chinese to mark them off as a large, distinct (and successful) minority group in Thailand.

7 To Singapore and Malaya

In Thailand the Chinese were able to blend into the host population quite easily. The situation changed with twentieth-century ideas of nationalism and the movement of Chinese

Singapore and Malaysia.

CHINA

BURMA

LAOS

THAILAND

VIETNAM

CAMBODIA

PHILIPPINES

PENANG

MALAYSIAN PENINSULAR

Malacca

SINGAPORE

SUMATRA

BORNEO

SULAWESI

NEW GUINEA

JAVA

AUSTRALIA

NEW ZEALAND

women to Thailand. Then their presence in the country was less welcome to the Thais.

Singapore and the other areas lining the Strait of Malacca came to be called the Straits Settlements. Unlike in Thailand, the Chinese who came to these settlements were easily distinguished from the much darker-skinned Malay peoples. Another difference was that almost all the Chinese migration came when the area was under colonial rule, either by the Portuguese, the Dutch or the British.

Malacca was a small Malayan kingdom which was conquered by the Portuguese in 1511. A short while afterwards a Portuguese writer, Tomé Pires, said:

> All the Chinese eat pigs, cows, and all other animals. They drink a fair amount of all sorts of beverages. They praise their wine greatly. They get pretty drunk. They are weak people, of small account. Those who are to be seen in Malacca are not very truthful, and steal – that is the common people. They eat with two sticks, and the earthenware or china bowl in their left hand close to their mouth with the two sticks to suck in. This is the Chinese way.
>
> (Tomé Pires, *The Suma Oriental of Tomé Pires*, tr. A. Cortesão, London, 1944, p. 116)

Perhaps the most interesting part of this description is that Pires thought the Chinese were "of small account". Not many other writers have agreed with him.

Nearly 300 years later, in 1785, the island of Penang was acquired by Britain. Its founder, Francis Light, did not underrate the Chinese. He wrote:

> The Chinese constitute the most valuable part of our inhabitants; they are men, women, and children, about 3,000, they possess the different trades of carpenters, masons, and smiths, are traders, shopkeepers and planters, they employ small vessels and prows and send adventurers to the surrounding countries. They are the only people of the east from whom a revenue may be raised without expense and extraordinary efforts of government.
>
> (Francis Light, "Notices of Pinang", *Journal of Indian Archipelago*, Vol. 5, 1850, p. 9)

This is the reason why the Chinese were actively welcomed by the colonial powers – they created wealth for themselves and in the process made money for their rulers. Light goes on to say:

> They are indefatigable in the pursuit of money, and like the Europeans, they spend it in purchasing those articles which gratify their appetites. They don't wait until they have acquired a large fortune to return to their native country, but send annually a part of their profits to their families. This is so general that a poor labourer will work with double labour to acquire two or three dollars to remit to China.

Not long after the founding of Penang, the island of Singapore was acquired by Sir Stamford Raffles. The first junk from China arrived there in 1821, only two years afterwards, and even before that other Chinese had moved in from Penang and Malacca. Raffles himself wrote:

The statue of Sir Stamford Raffles in Singapore.

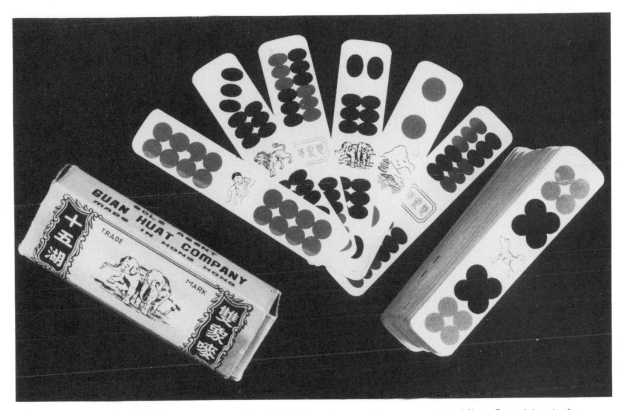

Chinese gambling cards. There are many different kinds, and many other ways of gambling. One visitor in the nineteenth century saw a fruit-seller gambling with his customers on the number of pips they would find in their oranges when they ate them.

My new colony thrives most rapidly. We have not been established four months, and it has received an accession of population exceeding 5,000 – principally Chinese, and their number is daily increasing.

(Raffles to Duchess of Somerset, 11 June 1819)

The colony did indeed thrive rapidly. By the 1980s there were nearly two million Chinese there, making up about 77 per cent of the total population. In the rest of the Malayan peninsula there were another six million Chinese, about 40 per cent of the population.

As in Thailand, there were several different speech groups involved in the migration. A late nineteenth-century writer says that the Hokkien were the wealthiest group. They were mostly shopkeepers and merchants, who used their capital to acquire profitable land which had been opened up by other Chinese. The Hakka and Teochiu were carpenters, miners, blacksmiths, shoemakers and other skilled tradesmen. Talking of the Hokkien, he writes:

They are great gamblers and most of the gaming houses are conducted by them. When a Cantonese contracts the habit of gambling, he is the more inveterate of the two, stakes higher and will play for all he possesses. He is looked for eagerly in the halls by the Hokkien who are cool and wary.

(J.D. Vaughan, *The Manners and Customs of the Chinese of the Straits Settlements*, Singapore, 1879 and 1971, p. 14)

Nearly a hundred years later, things were much the same:

The natives of Kwangtung (the Cantonese and Hakkas) were considered to be more robust than the Hokkiens and Teochius. They made the best squatters and pioneers in opening up the land. . . . Unfortunately they had no capital and had to get advances from their friends. The usual purchasers of the land were Hokkiens or Teochius. Most of the plantations which came into the hands of shopkeepers of these tribes, through the default of debtors

who owed them money, had been started by Cantonese. All the carpenters, blacksmiths, and shoemakers were Cantonese.

(Victor Purcell, *The Chinese in Southeast Asia*, 2nd edition, London, 1965, p. 248)

According to the 1947 Census of Singapore the speech groups were divided roughly as follows:

Hokkien	40%
Cantonese	22%
Teochiu	22%
Hainanese	7%
Hakka	6%
Others	3%

Over the years most of the Chinese who went to the Straits area eventually returned to China. Those who stayed often married Malay or Indian

---

Communication problems

An example of problems caused by the different speech groups can be found in a short autobiography written by a Singapore Chinese. At the age of 15 he was taken on as an assistant in a greengrocery business. He was sent out to collect and deliver orders from Westerners' houses.

My only languages were Teochiu and Mandarin. I could not speak English, nor could I understand a word of Singapore's many other languages. Most of the foreign houses had amahs [women servants] who were either Cantonese or from Hainan, and I was specially frightened of them, not being able to understand a word of what they said. Also, with every word they spoke they seemed to be shouting at me. Because of this I could not bring myself to answer them in Teochiu or Mandarin.

I turned helplessly to my colleague. "When I come here on my own, what language am I going to speak to them in?" My friend replied nonchalantly: "Just learn two words of English – "Good morning" and "Order". That'll be enough. It doesn't matter if it's the customer herself or the amah. Just use those two words."

(Tan Kok Seng, *Son of Singapore: the Autobiography of a Coolie*, Singapore, 1972, p. 48)

Babas

The Chinese are so attached to the habits of their forefathers, that notwithstanding an intercourse in the Straits for many generations with natives of all countries they have zealously adhered to their ancient manners and customs. . . .

One may see in Malacca *Babas* who can claim no connection with China for centuries, clad in long jackets, loose drawers, and black skull-caps, the very counterparts of Chinese to be seen any day at Amoy, Chusan, or under the walls of Nankin. . . .

It is well known to the *Baba* that the queue [pigtail] is a badge of servitude; that it was imposed upon the Chinese by their Manchu conquerors and that there is a strict law in China that the natives must shave their heads and wear tails, and not wear their hair loose and flowing according to ancient custom. . . . One would imagine that the *Babas*, and the natives of China themselves, when they got away from the thraldom [domination] of their Tartar rulers, would gladly avail themselves of their liberty and discard the queues, but such is not the case; you can offer no greater insult to a *Baba* than to cut his tail off, or even to threaten to do so.

(J.D. Vaughan, *The Manners and Customs of the Chinese of the Straits Settlements*, pp. 2-3)

---

or other non-Chinese wives. The children of such marriages were known as *Babas*, and eventually all Chinese not born in China were called *Babas* too. They spoke Malay or English but dressed as Chinese and mostly kept to Chinese custom. They were a distinct group in society, and have been called the "local aristocracy".

In Thailand the children of mixed Chinese-Thai marriages soon became more Thai than Chinese. They were influenced by their mothers rather than by their fathers. But in Malaysia and Singapore the father's influence was greater, and the children, the *Babas*, did not get absorbed by the non-Chinese population.

By the mid-nineteenth century some of the Chinese had become very prosperous under colonial rule. Here is a description from Singapore in the 1860s:

The Chinese merchant is generally a fat, round-faced man with an important and business-like look. He wears the same style of clothing (loose white smock, and blue or black trousers) as the meanest coolie, but of finer materials, and is always clean and neat; and his long tail tipped with red hangs down to his heels. He has a handsome warehouse or shop in town and a good house in the country. He keeps a fine horse and gig, and every evening may be seen taking a drive bareheaded to enjoy the cool breeze. He is rich, he owns several retail shops and trading schooners, he lends money at high interest and on good security, he makes hard bargains and gets fatter and richer every year.

(R. Wallace, *The Malayan Archipelago*, London, 1869, Vol. 1, pp. 32-3)

Not all Chinese were rich. A list of their occupations is given in a late-nineteenth-century book. It starts as follows:

The Chinese are everything: they are actors, acrobats, artists, musicians, chemists and druggists, clerks, cashiers, engineers, architects, surveyors, missionaries, priests, doctors, schoolmasters, lodging house keepers, butchers, porksellers, cultivators of pepper and gambier, cake-sellers, cart and hackney carriage owners, cloth hawkers, distillers of spirits, eating house keepers, fishmongers, fruitsellers, ferrymen, grass-sellers, hawkers, merchants and agents, oilsellers, opium shopkeepers, pawnbrokers, pig dealers, and poulterers.

(J.D. Vaughan, *The Manners and Customs of the Chinese of the Straits Settlements*, Singapore, 1879 and 1971, p. 15)

The list goes on to more than three times this length and many of the occupations are only poorly paid. The fact is that in Singapore and Penang the Chinese were in the majority and they were found at all levels of wealth and poverty. The rich could be very rich and the poor very poor. Just as in Thailand, some men didn't ever make the money they hoped for, and they

The Chinese in the Straits Settlements

They are by far the most industrious, and, consequently, the most valuable people we have in these possessions – the development of the internal resources of which is almost entirely due to them. . . . Unlike the Malays, they are ambitious and become rich. . . .

The proportion, however, of those who may be said to have permanently settled down is small, and the yearly addition to the Chinese population from birth altogether insignificant. The number is kept up entirely by immigration. During the months of December, January, February, March and April, fleets of junks crammed with Chinese coolies arrive at all the ports in the Straits from the different provinces of China. In Singapore the arrivals for the first four months of the present year (1864) were 8,560 males and 109 females – and for the whole year about 14,000, which is not much above the average of other years. Were this immigration in no way counterbalanced, the Chinese population of the Straits would soon become enormous, but it may be estimated that those who yearly return to China number quite two-thirds of the arrivals.

(J. Cameron, *Our Tropical Possessions in Malayan India*, 1865, pp. 139-40)

Bukit China ("The Hill of the Chinese") lies close to the heart of Malacca. It was bought as a graveyard for the Chinese in the seventeenth century and there are now about 12,500 graves on it. Of course, many other Chinese dead were sent back to China for burial.

either went home penniless or stayed on in lowly jobs to die where their hopes had died before them.

Apart from trading of all types, the Chinese were particularly active in farming and tin-mining and rubber plantation work. Chinese tin miners began to explore the land and hills from the start of the nineteenth century and they had almost a complete monopoly of the mining until a hundred years later. Their methods of work were simple and mainly consisted of washing the tin deposits out of soil dumped into water channels.

> Open-cast mining by hand labour is a purely Chinese method. *Dulang* washing, or panning, is a method employed for obtaining tin ore in many parts of the country. The work was done by Chinese women, usually Hakkas. A shallow wooden dish, about 30 inches in diameter and 3½ inches deep in the centre, was dug into the sand of the sluice or stream bed and a quantity of sand and water was scooped into it. The dish was then subjected to a peculiar motion by which the waste material was washed over the edge and the ore remained.

> *Dulang* washers were a fairly common sight in Malaya and were a striking reminder of the toughness of the Chinese. The women were bent double for hours in the heat of the sun, often immersed to the knees in water, and often with a baby strapped to their backs!
> (V. Purcell, *The Chinese in Southeast Asia*, second edition, London 1965, pp. 283-4)

When the world price of tin rose, Western companies began to open up mines in the same areas. These companies used much more machinery, but still a lot of the workers were Chinese. From tin many Chinese moved on to rubber-planting, especially after the beginning of the twentieth century when the motor industry created a worldwide demand for rubber. Other crops were grown in the seven years while the rubber trees reached productive age. In some places the Chinese settled as farmers, growing rice or vegetables for the tables of the people of the expanding towns and cities.

Until the 1920s, just as in Thailand, the number of Chinese women who emigrated to Singapore and Malaya was very small.

A Chinese open-cast tin mine in the early years of the twentieth century.

A Chinese immigrant family in Singapore at the beginning of the twentieth century.

A Chinese Success Story

Laurence K.L. Siaw in his book *Chinese Society in Rural Malaysia*, Kuala Lumpur, 1983, records the history of Siow Kon Chia, a Hakka from Guangdong Province. He left China on a "free" ticket and arrived in Malacca in 1892. He worked off his passage money in two years by doing odd jobs in mines and shops, then moved inland from the coast. Here he met some Roman Catholic missionaries and was converted to Christianity. With their help he began to operate several tin mines.

When he was short of labourers he wrote back to his old village, and whole families of his relatives migrated to join him. While the men did the tin-mining the women and children grew food and did other jobs. Kon Chia became very wealthy. Later, when tin became less profitable, he opened up rubber plantations instead and gave special help to his relatives who wanted to change too. He also started fruit- and vegetable-farming.

Kon Chia's wealth and position as "godfather" to so many Chinese families made him a much respected man and the British colonial government treated him as an unofficial leader of the community. When he died in 1929 at the age of 65 he had lived to see over a thousand families from his old homeland settled in the district which he had created almost single-handed.

Like *Nanyang* Chinese everywhere, the Sanchun Chinese were predominantly male. An elderly pharmacist recalls seeing only eight or ten Chinese women in the town when he arrived fifty years ago, but in any case women in those days would not have ventured out in public very often. Most shopkeepers had originally come to Sanchun as single laborers, saving their wages until they could begin small businesses. If business went well, they might eventually return to China for a bride or write for one to be sent. Since the actual selection was left to the man's parents, a mail-order bride was as good as any other, and cheaper.

(Judith Strauch, *Chinese Village Politics in the Malaysian State*, London, 1981, p. 54)

Some men, as we have seen, married non-Chinese women, but most were unmarried. Of course this meant that the men had no family life, but we have seen in Chapter Three that family life was very important to the Chinese. One way to make up for having no family was to go in for "imitation families". The men created imitation families through secret societies.

Secret Societies

Secret societies were formed by swearing oaths of brotherhood between men. Usually blood was spilled, mixed and drunk to show that all were now members of one family. Here are a few of the Thirty Six Oaths sworn by new members of the Hong Society, usually called the Triad Society.

A member must not thoughtlessly break a law, nor may he do harm to a Brother, be a covetous person, or a receiver of bribes. If any Brother do so offend, may he within one month be stabbed to death by a million knives.

A member must not seduce the wife of a Brother. If any member dare to break this law he shall be expelled from the Order, and may he die by being drowned in the Ocean.

Brothers must not take pen and paper and write indiscreet letters which will harm a Brother. If any disregard this rule may he die under the knife and his dismembered body be scattered here and there.

Having performed the ceremonies, on returning home a Brother must not sell the signs and secrets of the Hung Brotherhood. If any Brother be so shameless, may he be killed by a tiger or have his eyes bitten out by a snake.

(J.S.M. Ward and W.G. Stirling, *The Hung Society*, London, 1925, Vol. 1, pp. 65-7)

The punishments which were to fall on those who broke their secret society vows included death by drowning, by snake bite, by tiger-mauling, by many knives, by vomiting all their blood, by losing blood through all the seven holes of the head (eyes, nostrils, ears and mouth), by being blasted by lightning, by hanging, and by being blinded and drowned. The last of the 36 oaths ends:

If anyone be so brazen as to break any of these laws, may he die by losing his blood from the seven apertures, or be drowned in the Great Ocean & his body lost for ever. May the Spirits of his Ancestors be cursed and damned, and may his progeny exist in the deepest misery and want for a thousand generations.

Then at the swearing-in ceremony the new member had to chop off the head of a white cockerel, the blood was put in a bowl and mixed with blood taken from the man's finger and the fingers of other Brothers being sworn in. Finally all took a sip from it.

Signs used by secret members in a fight. The man's face is covered so that he cannot be identified and punished by his society for giving away its secrets.

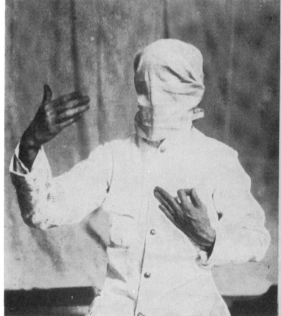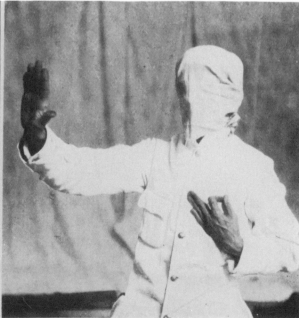

In China the family was the group which was closest to a man. When he needed help he turned first to his relations. In Malaysia and Singapore he had no family, so he turned to his imitation family, the secret society. If he was involved in a fight his brother members would take his side. If the society wanted help he in turn must be prepared to give it.

The secret societies were originally formed to oppose the rule of the Manchus in China, but by the end of the nineteenth century they were more often than not just gangs of men who were out to get what they could for themselves through their combined strength. Not all secret societies were criminal, but most of them were.

The organization of the emigration to the Nanyang was often done by secret societies. When the new migrant got off the boat he had little choice but to join the society which had brought him to his new land. The society was rather like a trades union, and it might not allow non-members to work in the trade which it controlled. This was particularly true of tin-mining, which was run by the secret societies.

In remote areas, such as the hills and inland valleys where tin-mining was carried on, the societies were the only means of organization there were, and they acted almost like local governments. They were not at first illegal or thought to be dangerous to law and order. But after some years there came to be serious rivalries between different societies which made the colonial government less favourable towards them.

In 1862 fighting broke out between members of two rival societies in Larut, Malaya. They both wanted to control the tin-mining there, and each wanted to stop the other from getting the scarce water supplies which were needed for the mines. Unfortunately, one of the societies had Cantonese members and the other had mainly Hakka membership. The two sides were made extra hostile because their organizations were based on two of the most important loyalties – love of the (imitation) family and love of speech group. The fighting lasted for ten years.

The loyalty to speech groups was shown in other ways, too. In major cities there were clubs or associations which were open to all who came from one speech group. There would be, for instance, a Teochiu Association. Such clubs were not like secret societies and did not have mystic entry rituals. Even so, they may from time to time

The "Five Counties" Speech Group Association headquarters in present-day Malacca. The columns of writing on each side of the door are good luck slogans.

have acted as the rallying point for speech group fighters. In 1854 there was a fierce riot in Singapore between the Hokkiens on one side and the Cantonese, Hakkas, Teochius and Hainanese on the other. Four hundred Chinese were killed. In 1870 and 1872, and again in 1876, there were vicious riots involving the Hokkiens and the Teochius.

Secret societies were made illegal in 1889, but they were not wiped out. Speech group associations were still legal, as were surname associations. Surname associations welcomed anyone with the same surname as a member. The Wang Surname Association was open to everyone surnamed Wang, the Li Surname Association to all Lis, and so on. These were also forms of "imitation families", based on the idea that all people with the same surname are related to each other, whether they know it or not. They were more like social clubs than anything else.

45

Buddhist priests sprinkle holy water on visitors to a "festival for peace" in Kuala Lumpur. Both Chinese and Indian believers flock to such festivals.

A Chinese temple in modern Singapore. It caters for the popular religion and is dedicated to a god called "Old Great Uncle".

Chinese Religion

In China, the three loyalties were backed up by different religious practices. Overseas, none of these was particularly appropriate. What the Chinese of Singapore and Malaya practised was what might be called "popular religion", a hotch-potch of Buddhism and nature-worship with spirit-mediums and fire-walking and various kinds of magic thrown in.

> If a Chinese in Singapore is asked what religion he follows he may be somewhat puzzled, since sectarian differentiation [division into religious groups] is not an important question to him. Only very rarely will a person answer that he is a Confucianist, and if he does so it will probably imply that he follows no sort of religious practice very closely. . . . On the other hand, many will claim to be Buddhists. This means that they or their womenfolk indulge fairly frequently in worship, although not necessarily of a Buddhist character. The probability, however, is that the answer will simply be "*pai shen*" – "I worship the gods".
>
> (A.J.A. Elliot, *Chinese Spirit-Medium Cults in Singapore*, London, 1955, p. 27)

All these societies became less important when the number of Chinese women migrants increased. Men then had more normal, settled home lives and were not as attracted by the excitements of activities involving men only.

The Chinese who went to Malaya and Singapore found themselves in a colonial state where they were encouraged to prosper. They were on more or less equal terms with the Malay people who were not in control of their own territory.

They had no families, but they created imitation ones. They had no speech group area, but they formed speech group clubs instead. They were out of China, but they were still sure that what was Chinese was best, and many of them went back to China alive or dead.

In Thailand there were no great religious differences between Chinese and Thais. Malayans, however, are Muslims, so that the Chinese were marked off from them by religion as well as by culture, language and skin colour.

Chinese ancestor tablets on an altar in a temple in Malacca. Each tablet houses the soul of a dead man or woman, or in some cases of a dead married couple. The descendants worship by burning incense and making offerings of food.

Footbinding

For more than a thousand years, until the 1930s, the women of China were crippled by footbinding. At the age of five or six the four small toes of each foot were drawn back under the foot by a figure 8 bandage tied round the heel. The foot was unable to grow, and eventually the arch would break leaving the damaged foot very small. The Chinese found this beautiful, but it was a barbaric and dangerous process. Luckily twentieth century Chinese men and women revolted against the custom, and now only a few old ladies with bound feet can be seen.

An old lady still with bound feet, photographed in China in 1985. Once the feet had been bound it was sometimes even more painful to leave the bandages off, and that is why examples like this can still be found.

This perhaps helps to explain the extraordinary length of time through which the Chinese have managed to stay a separate group. In 1879 Vaughan wrote:

> **In Malacca the Chinese were found when the Portuguese first made their appearance in these waters more than three hundred years ago, and they have been permanently settled there for many generations; and in Penang and Singapore they have been settled ninety and sixty years respectively, and yet they remain unchanged. One custom however has been entirely abandoned, viz., the barbarous practice of crushing the feet of girls and making them small-footed.**
>
> (J.D. Vaughan, *The Manners and Customs of the Chinese of the Straits Settlements*, Singapore 1879 and 1971, pp. 3-4)

8 To Australia

Australia had been opened up with cheap labour – convicts transported from Britain. But when transportation ceased in 1840 there was an immediate shortage of men to work on the farms

Australia and New Zealand.

CHINA

BURMA

LAOS

THAILAND

VIETNAM

CAMBODIA

PHILIPPINES

MALAYSIAN
PENINSULAR

SUMATRA

BORNEO

SULAWESI

NEW
GUINEA

JAVA

Northern
Territory

Queensland

Western
Australia

AUSTRALIA

South
Australia

New South
Wales

Victoria

Sydney

Melbourne

NEW ZEALAND

Early Chinese Arrivals

Before the *Nimrod* brought the first cargo of contract migrants to Sydney, a few Chinese had already been seen in Australia. They were so few that one author has made a note of who they were:

1827 Queng and Tchiou, cabinet makers in Sydney, were employed by John Dunmore Lang.

1836 John Acqu, a cabinet maker, arrived at Melbourne in 1836 and was naturalized in 1856.

1838 John Affoo, of Melbourne, a digger, arrived in Australia in 1838 and was naturalized in 1857.

1838 A Chinese was buried in the Old Cemetery, Melbourne, in 1838.

1842 Green, owner of Cricketers' Arms, Pitt Street, Sydney, imported two Chinese as house servants in his tavern.

1842 Tin Sang was tendered for the making of office furniture for the Custom House, Adelaide, in 1842.

1843 Wang Ah Hae, a carpenter, arrived in Melbourne in 1843 and was naturalized in 1854.

1844 John Alloo, a storekeeper, arrived at Sydney in 1844, left Sydney for Victoria in 1852, and was naturalized in 1856.

1847 John A. Hong Boney, a Chinese headman, arrived at Swan River, Western Australia, from Singapore in 1847, from thence to Adelaide in 1854, and left Adelaide for Melbourne in the same year; he was naturalized in 1859.

1848 *London*, a barque with seven Chinese, left Hong Kong via Manila and arrived at Sydney on March 16, 1848.

(Sing-wu Wang, *The Organization of Chinese Emigration 1848-1888*, San Francisco, 1978, pp. 263-4)

A Four-Year Contract

Here is part of the seven-clause agreement signed in 1848 between a Chinese labourer hired in Singapore and his Australian employers.

Singapore, 18th September, 1848

1. Yeh or Chong soe hereby agrees to serve Niel Black and Co. for four years, commencing from the date of arrival in Port Phillip, as Shepherd Hutkeeper or to be otherwise generally useful. Yeh promises to perform all the lawful and reasonable commands of the said Niel B. and Co. or of any Overseer they may place over him.

2. In consideration of the above mentioned services being duly performed by Yeh the said Yeh is to receive from the said Niel B. and Co. wages at the rate of Five dollars sixty cents per month, the dollar to be considered of the value of Four shillings and two pence sterling English money.

3. Yeh agrees that a monthly stoppage of One dollar and sixty cents (6s 8d. stg.) during the whole time of this agreement, be made from his pay and retained in the hands of Niel B. and Co. in liquidation of the cost of the passage of the said Yeh to Port Phillip and back to Singapore on completion of this agreement. Niel B. and Co. agree to find a passage and food during such passage for the said Yeh to Port Phillip, likewise a passage back to Singapore at the termination of this agreement, or so soon after as an opportunity may offer. . . .

4. Yeh agrees to furnish himself with necessary clothes and to have always in his possession or to allow a stoppage to be made from his pay, to purchase the following articles, namely: 1 pair blankets, 1 great coat, 1 wollen shirt, 1 pair strong trousers, 1 jacket, 1 pair boots.

5. Niel Black and Co. agree to supply Yeh with the following weekly ration of food in addition to the pay before mentioned, namely: 7lbs fresh meat, 8lbs wheat flour (or 10lbs rice in lieu of flour): 3oz tea, 1½lbs sugar, likewise cooking pots.

(P.L. Brown, ed., *Clyde Company Papers*, Vol. 4, London, 1941-63, pp. 413-14)

and sheep stations. For a while it looked as though India would supply the men, but the East India Company could not agree with the colonial governments on reasonable working conditions. So Australia looked further east to China.

The first ship to arrive in Sydney with Chinese contract labourers on board was the *Nimrod* in 1848. It had sailed from Amoy and carried 120 passengers, taking three months to make the voyage. For the next three years most of the migrants were Hokkien-speaking, leaving from Amoy or Singapore. By 1851 nearly 2000 men had made the journey to Australia.

Dramatically, in 1851, gold was discovered in

Gold Mountains

California had been known as Gold Mountains (*Jin Shan*) and when Australia became famous for gold too the Chinese were faced with the problem of what to call it. They named it New Gold Mountains (*Xin Jin Shan*) and California became Old Gold Mountains (*Jiu Jin Shan*). The names have stuck and are still used by Chinese today.

Chinese gold-miners, 1870.

New South Wales and Victoria. When the news reached the China coast, the fever brought on by the opening of the Californian gold-fields in America was at its height. The main flood of migrants carried on towards California, but after a while another stream began to head for Australia. In April 1854 the Hong Kong newspaper, the *China Mail*, reported:

> . . . within the last three months, upwards of 2100 have departed for Melbourne, thus showing what attention Australia is exciting among the Chinese; that Chinese passage brokers, being under such heavy engagements to find passages, are driven to the utmost straits, so that European ships condemned years ago as unfit to carry cargo are readily purchased at enormously high prices and fitted out for passages.

The way in which so many Chinese managed to get to Australia was by the credit-ticket system which had been developed for other migrations:

> A Chinese merchant in Australia, for instance, wants eight hundred or ten hundred coolies for the gold diggings: he sends the order to his merchant-friend in Hong Kong who procures the coolies, charters the steamer, and despatches her with the people. . . . There is no difficulty in getting the coolies; any well-reputed laborer is eligible, and the real trouble is to prevent too many getting aboard. . . . On arrival at Australia the coolie is received by the merchant who sent the order, and is put to work under Chinese foremen. Deductions are made from his earnings until the cost of his introduction has been refunded. There is no written contract and no recourse to the law courts. The whole transaction from beginning to end is arranged by the Chinese in their own peculiar fashion to the mutual profit, no doubt, of both merchant and laborer. Though there is no visible contract on paper, the employer does not hesitate to advance the costs, as he feels confident there will be no evasion or breach of the verbal agreement by the coolie. No people other than the Chinese could manage an extensive emigration on such a loose basis.

(From a letter written by H.A. Firth, an emigration official in Calcutta, 10 July 1875)

The gold-rush migration mostly came from Hong Kong and Macau, and this meant that the Chinese who ended up in Australia were nearly all Cantonese-speaking. There was not the same variety of speech groups that we saw in Thailand and Malaya. Even so, there were dialect differences within Cantonese which were enough to mark off one group from another. The largest groups were the men who came from the Sze Yap ("Four Counties") area to the south-west of Canton and those who came from the Sam Yap ("Three Counties") around Canton itself. These dialect groups did not specialize in particular work, so there was not much to make the differences stronger, and there was very little in the way of fighting or hostility between them. It was quite unlike the situation in Malaya and Singapore.

The Chinese gold-miners, or "diggers" as they were called, tended to keep apart from the men of European origin. They were physically less strong than the Europeans, and they were often "muscled" off the better mining areas.

> For clothing they wore full coloured trousers, loose jackets, pig-tails and large umbrella-like rattan hats sometimes six feet wide; even when adopting Australian dress – digger's hat and jacket, moleskin trousers and heavy boots – their trot came down to 'slow dragging pace' that, with their oriental features and pig-tails, still distinguished them clearly from the European population.... When on a gold-field they pitched tents, stacked with strange-looking cooking utensils on the outside and coloured prints on the inside, in orderly 'villages' well apart from the Europeans; larger villages contained their own Chinese stores, butcheries, restaurants and occasionally banks....
>
> (Charles A. Price, *The Great White Walls Are Built*, Canberra, 1974, p. 81)

> The first reaction to Chinese diggers was one of amused curiosity. There was an interest in the customs of the Chinese, a desire to know something of their ways, perhaps to learn from them. Vistors thronged around the Chinese encampment on the banks of the Yarra while Chinese demonstrated the art of using chopsticks and of winding their queues [pigtails].... 'Almost every person' was reported to have paid a visit to their encampment. The economical use of fire-wood by the Chinese was favourably commented upon.
>
> (Andrew Markus, *Fear and Hatred*, Sydney, 1979, p. 237)

Later, as more and more Chinese flocked to the gold-fields, the Europeans began to be alarmed at their numbers, and soon the "amused curiosity" gave way to jealousy, resentment and persecution. This change of view was not just a result of racial prejudice: it was partly due to the fact that as each gold-field opened up, the easily mined gold was quickly worked out, so that earlier miners were already afraid for their livelihood almost as soon as the Chinese began to appear on the scene.

Chinese men eating with chopsticks.

In 1855 the parliament in Victoria passed an act to control Chinese immigration. Each Chinese had to pay £10 as a landing fee. In addition, it was made illegal for any ship to carry and land more

The Chinese in California

In the 1850s and 1860s a tidal wave of Chinese surged into California in pursuit of a dream. The newcomers came with a vision: they would make money to return to China with their savings for a life of ease, surrounded and honoured by the families which their toil had sustained. Their goal kept the Chinese apart from the flood of other immigrants who came to America as permanent residents.

(Gunter Barth, *Bitter Strength: a History of the Chinese in the United States*, Cambridge, Mass., 1964, p. 1)

Often, an American miner puzzled over the strange sight of the blue-clad men with great broad hats and swinging queues, with their bundles and packs, their picks and shovels, dangling from poles across their shoulders. The miner spotted them marching one behind the other on a nearby trail. When he learned that these men were Chinese he laconically observed that they were here and that was that...

(Gunter Barth, *Bitter Strength*, p. ix)

This early tolerance was rapidly changed to fear and dislike, just as in Australia.

Chinese migrants landing in Australia, 1877. (From the Illustrated Australian News, *9 July 1879)*

than one Chinese for every ten tons registered tonnage of the ship itself. The result was that ships' captains landed their immigrants in South Australia colony instead, and the Chinese then walked overland into the gold-fields of Victoria:

> **I met between six and seven hundred coming overland from Adelaide. They had four wagons carrying their sick, lame, and provisions. They were all walking single file, each one with a pole and two baskets. They stretched for over two miles in procession. I was half an hour passing them.**
>
> (J. Chandler, *Forty Years in the Wilderness*, Hartwell, 1893, pp. 70-1)

It is said that nearly 14,500 Chinese entered Victoria by this method in the first six months of 1857 alone.

It was around this time that a series of major clashes began in the colony of Victoria. About 2000 Chinese miners were chased off the land by riotous Europeans. They beat up and robbed the Chinese, burned their tents and their temple, and threw all their belongings into the river. Although the police eventually regained control and persuaded the Chinese to return, only four Europeans were found guilty in court. The incident was fairly typical of what went on throughout the gold-rush. The Chinese were feared, intimidated and given unfair treatment by the Europeans.

The Chinese were accused of bringing leprosy and smallpox into Australia, of living in filthy and disgusting conditions which were inhuman, of spoiling the water supplies for the other miners, of stealing the gold, which belonged by right to European-origin people, of corrupting European women with opium so as to enslave them, of being homosexuals, and even of biting Europeans to death! Superstitious miners claimed that the mere presence of Chinese on a gold-field caused the gold to disappear.

Angus Cameron, a Sydney politician, said in 1880:

> **There is about the immorality of Chinamen a distinct and peculiar character which is more loathsome in a tenfold degree than the character of the Europeans' iniquities.**
>
> (A. Cameron, *New South Wales Parliamentary Debates*, June, 1880, p. 2896).

Other politicians were able to point out that it was not true that Chinese living conditions were worse than European slums, and that alcoholism and some other social evils were not found among the Chinese. But over the years the old charges were renewed and more and more controls were introduced.

In 1901 the Commonwealth of Australia was formed, and it immediately passed the Immigration Restriction Act. This Act was intended to keep out virtually all immigrants except those of White, European origin. It stopped others coming in by insisting on an "education test", which was a dictation of 50 words in a European language. The Secretary of the Department of External Affairs wrote in 1903:

It is not desirable that persons should be allowed to pass the test, and before putting it to anyone the Officer should be satisfied that he will fail. If he is considered likely to pass the test if put in English, it should be applied in some other languages of which he is ignorant.
(Atlee Hunt to Collector of Customs, Fremantle, 1903)

The act put an end to all but a trickle of Chinese migration. It also sparked off a small increase in illegal entry into the country.

The rise and fall in the numbers of Chinese in Australia tells the story very clearly:

A Chinese doctor and his servants in Australia. (From the Illustrated Australian News, *22 January 1879)*

1841	almost nil
1851	2,000
1861	38,300
1871	27,700
1881	38,700
1891	37,800
1901	32,700
1911	25,800
1921	20,800
1933	14,300
1947	12,100

One reason why numbers went down over the years was because so few Chinese women migrated to Australia. In 1861 there were only 11 Chinese women compared with over 38,000 men, and 40 years later, in 1901, there were still fewer than 500. This meant that there was little chance of the Chinese community maintaining its numbers through birth. It also meant that a lot of the men who had migrated went back to China to marry, or, if they had wives there already, they retired back to be with their families.

Another reason for the fall in numbers was the

Chinese Women in Australia			
1861	11	1911	840
1871	48	1921	1138
1881	259	1933	1528
1891	350 (approx.)	1947	2533
1901	474		

normal Chinese attitude to emigration. Many of the men had no intention of remaining overseas. They went only to make money and then they went home again. Most of them must have been very glad to leave, for the Europeans made it harder and harder for them to feel comfortable or to earn a good wage. Chinese gold-miners in Victoria had to pay a special licence fee, and by 1860 about 6000 of them had been fined or imprisoned for failure to pay it:

> Partly because of this, partly because many had been long enough in Australia to return home with substantial savings, and partly because the expanding New South Wales gold-fields were offering greater and unrestricted opportunities, numbers in Victoria started to decline. Nearly 10,000 returned to China 1857-9 (some with nearly £100)...
>
> (C.A. Price *The Great White Walls Are Built*, Canberra, 1974, pp. 73-4)

By the 1890s the numbers of Chinese in the gold-fields were small. Those who had not left Australia had spread to other occupations. They were seamen, cabinet-makers, sheep-men, cooks, servants, laundry-workers, tobacco-growers and market-gardeners. But unfair treatment continued, particularly where they were in competition with European labour, as was the case with cabinet-making, laundry-work, sheep-farming, sea-faring and market gardening. Matters were not improved when attempts were made by bosses to use Chinese labour to replace Europeans on strike, as happened in the gold-fields and on Australian ships.

All in all, the early migration to Australia was neither a happy nor a very successful one. The men lived unnatural, solitary lives, cut off from the benefits of family life, moved on from occupation to occupation, sneered at as the "yellow agony". There was little relaxation for them other than the dangerous excitement of gambling and the dreams and sleep brought on by smoking opium. By the end of the nineteenth century those who remained were concentrating in small "Chinatowns" in the cities, the old men being looked after by newly founded Chinese charities. Some men (such as Quong Tart, whose story was told at the beginning of this book) managed to fit in successfully with Australian life, but they were very few.

A new period of migration began in the mid-1950s. In ten years the Chinese population of Australia rose to about 30,000 and it has gone on growing since. By 1986 it was estimated that perhaps as many as 200,000 Chinese were living there. These later migrants have had an easier time of it. They have tended to live in the towns and cities, but scattered amongst the rest of the population rather than all together in Chinatowns. There are now as many women as men, and Chinese are to be found in all kinds of jobs and professions.

An Unhappy Migration

Here are some stories of Chinese migrants to New Zealand, where conditions were very similar to those in Australia.

> Newspapers of the earlier days give revealing accounts of the treatment of the Chinese, for the Press almost without exception referred to them as "Chinamen", "Celestials", "Johnny" or "John". The *Daily Telegraph*, June 2, 1863 described the scene of the first "Chinaman" in Dunedin. "His reception was noisy and appeared rather to disconcert Johnny, who took to his heels, and scudded up the street at a rapid pace." *The Otago Witness*, February 8, 1868 gave a pitiful picture of the only Chinese working at Naseby. A crowd of drunk hooligans cut off the pigtail of Ah Pack, stripped most of his clothes and closed him in a large cask and rolled the terrified man about town. The police took him into custody, but the man had partly gone out of his mind and wandered about the country looking for Chinese friends.
>
> In 1905, a spectacular murder spotlighted the Chinese question. Lionel Terry, an Englishman of considerable intelligence, shot dead an elderly Chinese whom he met. ... Terry wanted to draw attention to the danger of the "Yellow Peril" and ... said that "as a protest against immigration", he had "deemed it advisable to put to death a Chinaman that evening".
>
> (Ng Bickleen Fong, *The Chinese in New Zealand*, Hong Kong, 1959, p. 27)

Opium Smoking

Although the Chinese had known about opium for centuries they did not begin to smoke it until about 300 years ago. The habit was probably confined to only a very few people before the British East India Company began to ship large quantities of the drug to China in the early eighteenth century. Chinese going overseas took the habit with them, and Australia was no exception to the rule:

> Just imagine this picture! An opium den: the air thick with acrid smoke and men lying on the floor with the end of the opium pipe in their mouths; in some rooms men lie half-unconscious and quietly exhilerated. One smoker may be holding the bamboo pipe and drawing the opium smoke slowly into his lungs. His face is haggard; his body is thin and everytling about him is depressing. . . . The evils of opium are beyond question. Though opium-smoking may give the addict temporary pleasure and stimulation, it unquestionably does harm by absorbing the earnings of the smoker, sapping his physical strength and undermining his will and disposition to work.

(C.F. Yong, *The New Gold Mountain*, South Australia, 1977, p. 179)

A Chinese picture of an opium smoker, thin and in poverty.

Chinese men smoking opium in the 1890s.

9 Fitting in

The southward movement of the Chinese people did not stop at the coast of China. Settlers went with their families to the islands of Hainan and Taiwan and drew them into the Chinese empire. For centuries Hainan was considered an outpost of empire, and convicts were sent there from north China to live out sentences of exile. Taiwan was colonized later than Hainan, but became part of China in 1680.

A few Chinese had journeyed to South-East Asia to trade before the great Ming dynasty expeditions of Zheng He, and afterwards many more did so. They went to the islands of the Philippines, Indonesia and Borneo, and to Siam, Annam, Burma, Laos, Cambodia and Malaya on the mainland. Here, the pattern was different, for they were mostly not settlers but traders and workers who wanted to stay for a time only. One of their problems was that they were successful, and their prosperity was often envied by the other peoples of the area. In the Philippines this resulted in bloody massacres of the Chinese in 1603, 1639, 1763 and 1819. In other places there were attempts to make them live separately and to tax them especially hard.

The great bulk of Chinese movement overseas came in the late nineteenth and early twentieth centuries. What drove them overseas was the need to make a livelihood at a time when China was desperately poor and very overcrowded. The pull from the outside was the need of governments in developing nations for manpower.

There were countries all over the world which took Chinese labourers in this new round of migration. In Australia, New Zealand, South Africa, California and Canada it was gold which was the first attraction, but afterwards came work in market-gardening, railway construction, land clearance, laundries, hotels and restaurants. On the Pacific island of Nauru it was the phosphate diggings which drew Chinese labour. In Cuba and other West Indian and South American countries it was sugar and other plantations which needed labour to replace slaves. In South-East Asia the Chinese moved in as labourers or traders wherever local people were unwilling or unable to do the work themselves.

The migrations of the Chinese to some places were not much different from the Black slave migrations which by then most of the world had outlawed:

The Usefulness of the Chinese
The Chinese dominated the economy of the Philippines and suffered for it:

After the 1603 revolt the consequences were soon felt economically. Because of the massacre of the Chinese, food was not to be found nor even shoes, even when one was willing to pay very high prices. . . . The natives do not practise any trade, and have even forgotten how to cultivate their land and raise fowl, cattle and cotton and how to weave blankets. . . . Naturally, the Chinese were blamed, for their industry succeeded in making vagabonds out of the natives.
(L. Diaz-Trechuelo in Alfonso Felix, ed., *The Chinese in the Philippines*, Vol. 1, Manila, 1966, p. 183)

The importers of Chinese laborers were businessmen, and they were in the business for profit. They gave little attention to the physical aptitude of the Chinese for the work he was to perform, nor did they worry about his customs and characteristics. Neither was his comfort on the long voyage given much consideration. The ships that conveyed the coolies became known as "floating hells", and for very good reasons. While an English regulation published in 1853 to govern the movement of Chinese through Hong Kong allowed twelve square feet (two feet by six) for each man, it could be enforced only at Hong Kong, and in general only eight square feet were allotted, and overcrowding of the ships was the rule. To appreciate the seriousness of this fact, it is only necessary to observe that the voyage of some nine thousand miles from Macau to Callao, Peru's seaport, required in many cases 120 days of navigation. The mortality rate was extreme. In 1850, of 740 emigrants embarked on two ships for Callao, 247 died on the voyage, more than 33 per cent. The ship *Empresa* of 446 tons, which made the voyage from Amoy to Callao in 114 days, took aboard 323 Chinese, but when it reached Callao on November 7, 1852, it carried but 246. The other 77 – or almost 24 per cent – had died at sea.

(W. Stewart, *Chinese Bondage in Peru*, Connecticut, 1951, p. 18)

Even more horrifying was the import of large numbers of Chinese to South Africa to replace Black labour, which was felt to be too expensive and too much prone to fatal illness – in 1903-4 there was said to be a monthly death rate among Black mine-workers of 70 men in every thousand employed!

One form of punishment of Chinese was to handcuff them over a beam. The beam was too high to allow them to sit and the strain on the legs was very painful.

The Government admitted the danger of allowing 50,000 Chinamen to be planted down in a colony without any restrictions. Their introduction was a regrettable necessity, and so it was proposed to keep them in compounds, to round them up every night like sheep, to make them liable to heavy penalties if they wandered abroad without a permit. . . . It was pointed out to them that this would be semi-slavery, if not indeed actual slavery. The Chinaman was not to be employed in any position but that of a miner, he could not improve his position; he could not give notice to one employer and go to another. He could never leave the compound without per-mission. If he struck work [refused to work] he could be imprisoned. He was bound to reside on the premises of his employer, in charge of a manager appointed for the purpose. Permission to leave these premises might or might not be granted; but in any case he could never be absent for more than forty-eight hours at a time. If he escaped, he could be tracked down, arrested without a warrant and imprisoned by a magistrate. . .

('An English Eye Witness', *John Chinaman on the Rand*, London, 1905, pp. 32-3)

"If he escaped he could be tracked down". Hunting escaped Chinese coolies was a kind of sport to some men in South Africa.

So flourishing was the trade in people that it has been impossible to work out how many Chinese went overseas in this period: they went to so many different places, from so many different ports, and often they went illegally. One specialist, after going into the matter very thoroughly, was only able to make the following rough guess:

The number of Chinese emigrating abroad between 1840 and 1900 must be placed at close to the following figures:

Southeast Asia	1,545,000
West Indies & South America	400,000
The United States, Australia, New Zealand, and others	410,000
	2,355,000

(Sing-wu Wang, *The Organization of Chinese Emigration*, San Francisco, 1978, p. 9)

The picture is made more complicated, because many of those who went abroad returned to China, sometimes after only a few years, sometimes after a lifetime of hard work. But this two-way emigration was very important in shaping the style of the overseas Chinese communities. It meant that all the Chinese abroad, all *Hua-qiao*, remained interested in China and were comparatively uninterested in mixing with the cultures among which they were living. And of course they believed in any case that Chinese culture was the best.

A Chinese community cut off from China would no doubt eventually have blended in with the other people who lived there. This had begun to happen in Australia and New Zealand after Chinese immigration was restricted at the end of the nineteenth century. But most Chinese communities were not cut off from China and they were kept constantly supplied with new members fresh from the homeland.

The character of the Chinese has frequently been described, and no change of scene or circumstance seems materially to affect it. They have attained a high civilization of their own sort, and this keeps, and I think always will keep, them distinct from the other peoples with whom they mingle. I have met them in the most out-of-the-way islands in the Archipelago, where, perhaps, a dozen of them had formed a settlement, and had gradually monopolized the trade of a people numbering many thousands, without any concession in dress, in religion, or in manners; they were the same in every respect as are to be found in Java, in the Straits, and in the sea-ports of their own country.

(John Cameron, *Our Tropical Possessions in Malayan India*, London, 1865, pp. 140-1)

It was partly this reluctance to abandon their own culture that made the Chinese targets for jealousy and attack from other peoples:

In those days, instead of delivering in a truck, we had to carry the case or sack on our shoulder. Sometimes we had to walk a long way up the hill in all weathers. Not infrequently we were pushed over by people who wanted "some fun", our goods scattered in the street amidst a chorus of "Ching Chong Chinaman". It made our blood boil, but we kept our poker face. What else could we do? We were Chinese, we had no political protection and had to earn our living. We all longed for the time when we could go home and live in peace. That hope was the only thing that kept us going at times.

(Ng Bickleen Fong, *The Chinese in New Zealand*, Hong Kong, 1959, p. 97)

The *Hua-qiao* were involved in the politics of China as well as its culture. They tended to have little interest in the politics of the country in which they lived, and this was another cause of suspicion and fear of them by other peoples.

Towards the end of the nineteenth century revolutionary movements in China began to threaten the corrupt and weak Manchu government. The man who became leader of the revolutionaries was Dr Sun Yat-sen. He had been

Overseas Chinese

The movement abroad became so much a regular feature that the Chinese language has a special word for those Chinese who live overseas; it is *Hua-qiao*. The term *Hua-qiao* has sometimes been applied wrongly to Chinese living in Taiwan or Hong Kong, but it is correctly used of anyone of Chinese descent who lives more or less permanently abroad. Chinese businessmen on a trip abroad, or Chinese tourists, or Chinese embassy staff would not be considered *Hua-qiao*.

educated in Hong Kong and had lived in Hawaii, and he turned naturally to the *Hua-qiao* for help in financing his revolution. They responded generously.

> **The effect of this movement was ... to emphasize the detachment of the Chinese in Southeast Asia from the affairs of the countries in which they lived. The indigenous local peoples took no interest in the politics of China: the Chinese had no concern for the aspirations, now dawning, of the local nationalists. The view which saw the Chinese as alien sojourners [visitors] in foreign lands was strengthened by the obvious fact that the Chinese were politically interested only in the affairs of China.**
>
> (C.P. FitzGerald, *The Third China*, Melbourne, 1965, p. 22)

The revolution succeeded in 1911, and before long the Republican Government set up a Ministry of Overseas Chinese to look after the *Hua-qiao* who had been so helpful to them. The law of China now said "Once a Chinese always a Chinese"; and that meant that China now claimed a hold over everyone in the world who had Chinese blood. This made countries with Chinese immigrants even more distrustful of them. It is not surprising that Chinese communities have continued to be regarded as a problem in this century. In Indonesia there have been bloody persecutions of the *Hua-qiao*; in Malaya there was a long period of confrontation between Chinese and the British colonial forces after the Second World War; in Thailand laws discriminating against the Chinese have been passed – and so on.

The Hong Kong Cultural Services in London where many thousands of Hong Kong Chinese live and work.

Numbers of Overseas Chinese Today
It is very difficult to find an accurate figure for how many Overseas Chinese there are in the world. Based on a definition which assumes that *Hua-qiao* means all Chinese residing abroad, plus naturalized citizens of Chinese descent, plus descendants of wholly Chinese parents, there were probably some 27 million *Hua-qiao* by the end of 1985. About 90 per cent of these were in the countries of Asia, more than 6 per cent were in America, and just over 2 per cent in Europe. The remainder were scattered in Africa and the South Pacific region. (Figures projected from the *China Yearbook 1980*, Taibei, 1980, and the *Overseas Chinese Economy Year Book 1982-83*, Taibei, 1983)

There has also been a continuing small emigration of the Chinese. Since 1949, when the Chinese Communist Party came to power in China, the Chinese Government has made migration from the motherland very difficult. Migrants have come instead from Hong Kong, to a more limited extent from Taiwan, and most recently from Vietnam as the Chinese community there has sought refuge in other parts of the world.

This "third wave" of Chinese migration has planted new communities in most of the countries of the world, but in particular in the developed nations of Western Europe, in Canada, the United States and, once again, in Australia.

The remarkable spread of the Chinese around the world has, of course, led to problems. Before the twentieth century the Overseas Chinese were exposed to other cultures but remained true to Chinese culture. In this second half of the twentieth century Chinese culture itself has gone through great changes and has begun to move closer to Western patterns. It is likely that this will make it easier for Overseas Chinese communities to fit in with the peoples they live amongst.

But it would be a great pity if "fitting in" meant the disappearance of Chinese culture. Chinese philosophies are exciting for people from other countries. Chinese food has added new colour and flavours to eating habits everywhere. The skills and hard work of the Chinese have helped the economy of many countries. By retaining their "Chineseness" the *Hua-qiao* can greatly enrich the rest of the world.

Glossary

almanac the Chinese calendar, published every year. Gives information on both the lunar and solar year. Shows lucky and unlucky times for such things as house-building, getting engaged, meeting friends, and having a haircut.

Babas children of Chinese fathers and non-Chinese mothers; also fully Chinese people born in Malaya and Singapore who do not speak Chinese.

Cantonese people from the south China province of Guangdong, especially those from in and around the city of Guangzhou; also the Chinese language they speak.

credit-ticket system payment of the expenses of emigration by an employer overseas, who then deducts the money from the migrant's wages until the debt is repaid.

diggers gold-miners in Australia.

footbinding the tight bandaging of a Chinese girl's feet to prevent them growing. Small feet used to be considered particularly beautiful.

Hailam or Hainanese people from Hainan island off the south coast of China; also the Chinese language they speak.

Hakka usually people from inland Guangdong province, but Hakka people are found in various parts of south and central China; also the Chinese language they speak.

Hokkien people from Fujian province in south-east China; also the Chinese language they speak.

Hua-qiao the Chinese word for Chinese people living permanently overseas.

junk a Chinese-style ship, usually an ocean-going one.

Manchu the Manchu people ruled China from A.D. 1644 until 1912.

Nanyang the Chinese word for South-East Asia.

panning a method of washing gold or tin ore out of soil.

pigs Chinese who went overseas under the credit-ticket system.

queue a pigtail.

sampan a small Chinese boat.

slavers ships which carried slaves.

Teochiu people from the coast of eastern Guangdong province; also the language they speak.

Date List

1368-1644 The Ming dynasty rules China.

1405-33 Zheng He's fleets explore the southern oceans.

1644-1911 The Manchu Qing dynasty rules China.

1712 The Emperor decrees that leaving China is punishable by death.

1785 Penang comes under British rule.

1819 Sir Stamford Raffles founds Singapore.

1840 Convict transportation to Australia ends.

1842 The Treaty of Nanking ends the Opium War between China and Britain. Five Chinese ports are opened to international trade and Hong Kong is ceded to Britain.

1848 The *Nimrod* brings the first contract labourers to Australia.

1850-64 The Taiping Rebellion leaves much of China in ruins.

1851 Gold is discovered in Australia.

1853 Hong Kong attempts to control overcrowding of migrant ships.

1855 £10 landing fee imposed on Chinese in order to control immigration to Australia.

1859 Quong Tart moves to Australia.

1860 The Convention of Peking opens eleven more ports to trade.

1864 China decrees the death penalty for kidnappers.

1874 The Straits Settlements attempt to stop the overloading of migrant ships.

1887 Chinese officials visit Overseas Chinese in Australia.

1889 Secret societies are made illegal in the Straits Settlements.

1893 Leaving China is no longer illegal.

1901 Immigration Restriction Act is passed in Australia.

1904 Chinese coolies go to South Africa.

1912 The Republic of China is set up by Dr Sun Yat-sen.

1914-18 First World War. Coolies go to Europe.

1939-45 Second World War.

1942 Thailand passes laws limiting the jobs that Chinese can do.

1946-9 Civil war in China.

1949 The Chinese Communists defeat the Nationalists and set up the People's Republic of China.

1950- Emigration from Hong Kong to Western Europe, Australia and the Americas.

Book List

Garth Alexander, *Silent Invasion: the Chinese in Southeast Asia*, Macdonald, 1973
*Maurice Collis, *Foreign Mud*, Faber & Faber, 1946 and subsequent editions
Richard J. Coughlin, *Double Identity: the Chinese in Modern Thailand*, Hong Kong University Press, 1960
*Robert S. Elegant, *The Dragon's Seed: Peking and the Overseas Chinese*, St Martin's Press, 1959
C.P. Fitzgerald, *China: a Short Cultural History*, Cresset, 1935 and subsequent editions
C.P. Fitzgerald, *The Southern Expansion of the Chinese People*, Barrie & Jenkins, 1972
Ng Bickleen Fong, *The Chinese in New Zealand*, Hong Kong University Press, 1959
Andrew Markus, *Fear and Hatred*, Sydney, 1979
*Lois Mitchison, *The Overseas Chinese: a Background Book*, Bodley Head, 1961
W.P. Morgan, *Triad Societies in Hong Kong*, Hong Kong Government Printer, 1960 and subsequent editions
Ng Kwee Choo, *The Chinese in London*, Oxford (for Institute of Race Relations), 1968
C.A. Price, *The Great White Walls are Built*, Canberra, 1974

Victor Purcell, *The Chinese in Southeast Asia*, second edition, Oxford (for Royal Institute of International Affairs), 1965
*Anthony Shang, *The Chinese in Britain*, B.T. Batsford, 1984
G. William Skinner, *Chinese Society in Thailand*, Cornell University Press, 1957
*J.D. Vaughan, *The Manners and Customs of the Chinese of the Straits Settlements*, Singapore, 1879; reprinted Oxford, 1971
Sing-wu Wang, *The Organization of Chinese Emigration 1848-1888*, Chinese Materials Center Inc., 1978
James L. Watson, *Emigration and the Chinese Lineage: the Mans in Hong Kong and London*, California University Press, 1975
Myra Willard, *History of the White Australia Policy to 1920*, Melbourne 1923; reprinted Frank Cass, 1967
*C.F. Yong, *The New Gold Mountain*, South Australia, 1977

*indicates a book suitable for younger secondary school readers.

Picture Acknowledgments

The Author and Publishers would like to thank the following for their kind permission to reproduce illustrations: Alex R. Baker for page 38; Peter Y.L. Ng for page 21; United Reform Church Archive (School of Oriental and African Studies' Library) for pages 9 and 43; Wing King Tong Co. Ltd, Hong Kong for page 15.

Cover Illustrations
The colour photograph is of a Chinese junk; the black and white print shows Chinese gold-miners in Australia, 1870; the figure of the Chinese was drawn by Nick Theato.

Index